An American President in Ealing

The John Quincy Adams Diaries
1815–1817

Boston Lane - Little Ealing. — The family were engaged the whole
, with our baggage, furniture and Wines, to remove to this place - But
tantly engaged with company. Mr Hare, and a Mr Von Harten, a Ger
a and took Passports. Mr Nathaniel Amory paid me a visit; having
Mr Norman called. He arrived a few days since from Berlin, where
r American Sailors came to obtain passages to the United States, and
gave them a Letter to Mr Beasley - Mr Joy was with me from Noon,
clock; and shewed me Letters that he formerly received from Mr Marsh
ed the waggon and Carts were dispatched. Antoine went with them. Fu
id with my son John came out in the Carriage, which returned for us
ams, with our sons George and Charles, and myself, left the lodgings at
me out to this place, where we arrived between nine and ten in the E
d were all unloaded and the articles housed before Midnight

d all the Morning, in unpacking my trunks and in arranging my books
h we have taken is not large; but neat, and elegant, and fitted up with al
English domestic life. We have a Coach house and Stable, Dairy, Fruit an
and before dinner, I rode out with Mrs Adams to enquire for a school fo
Orgar House, at Acton, about two Miles from our own residence, where
a house, and enquired of the terms, but were not pleased with the resu
Nicholas at Ealing - not more than a Mile from our house and which had be
ool of 250 boys, and we were so well satisfied, upon enquiry and inspection
hat we engaged to send the two boys, as soon as we can get them prepared.
bout a Mile distant from our house — Mr Grubb sent me out by the three j
the last of June.

a unpacking of effects, and I made an arrangement of part of my Pape
66 sfeveral letters with applications for Passports. I went into town wit
m we found at home. Sir James was gone to town. We then went to hi

An American President in Ealing

The John Quincy Adams Diaries 1815–1817

Written and compiled by Duncan Cameron, Andrew Dick, Paul Fitzmaurice, Helen Johnson, Rosmarie Matter, Joyce Mistry, Rita Smith and Mary Woods, using extracts from the John Quincy Adams diaries courtesy of the Massachusetts Historical Society

Little Ealing
History Group

Designed by Colin Barker, Publications Workshop
Printed in China by Toppan Leefung
Published by Little Ealing History Group, Ealing, London
www.littleealinghistory.org.uk

First published 2014
British Library Cataloguing in Publication Data:
A catalogue record for this book is available from the British Library.

Cover: Ealing parish map 1822; portrait of John Quincy Adams by C. R. Leslie.
Frontispiece: Facsimile extract from the John Quincy Adams diaries.

FSC
www.fsc.org

MIX
Paper from
responsible sources
FSC® C104723

ISBN 978 0 9927679 0 7

Contents

Acknowledgements

The authors wish particularly to thank the Massachusetts Historical Society for their kind permission to reproduce extracts of the John Quincy Adams diaries from the Adams Papers and for their courtesy and helpfulness in dealing with our enquiries. Thanks are also due to the Bodleian Library in Oxford for their assistance in copying pages from the microfiche of the Adams diaries stored at the Library.

We have made many contacts in the United States, which have been very helpful in furthering our background knowledge of John Quincy Adams. We would particularly like to thank the late Marjorie Heffron and her English colleague Bettie McGurk, Ken Thomas, Mary Bondurrant Warren and Louisa Thomas. Probably the most remarkable overseas connection we made was with Joan Bellefeuille in Canada, through her daughter Sue. Joan, who sadly died in 2010, was able to provide photographs and her memories of living in Little Boston House as a child, immediately prior to its demolition in about 1930.

Special thanks go to Hounslow Heritage Guide Janet McNamara whose own detailed researches first alerted us to the fact that John Quincy Adams had lived in the locality and whose interest and encouragement have been a constant factor in the production of this book. Our thanks also go to the many other local people who have given us help and support; in particular, we would mention Carolyn Hammond of Chiswick Library, Jonathan Oates of Ealing Central Library, James Marshall of Hounslow Library, Vanda Foster of Gunnersbury Park Museum, David Shailes, and our sister organisation Ealing Fields Residents' Association.

Our final thanks must go to our spouses, partners and families for their patience and forbearance during the preparation of this book.

Introduction

John Quincy Adams was a leading nineteenth-century American statesman and diplomat. A serious man with a strong sense of public duty, he served his country with unswerving dedication from his teenage years to his old age, and was elected the sixth President of the United States in 1825. Between 1815 and 1817 he served as the United States representative in Great Britain and lived with his family at Little Boston House on the Boston Manor estate, now on the border of Ealing and Brentford in West London.

Throughout his life Adams kept a detailed diary, and the record of his two years in Ealing provides a fascinating insight, not only into his life and thought, but also into the life of the area in the early nineteenth century. In this book, using the diary and other sources, we explore the life of Adams and his family and the community in which they lived during their time in Britain.

Chapter 1

John Quincy Adams: his life and career

Early life

John Quincy Adams was born in July 1767, the second child of John and Abigail Adams, at the family home, a farmhouse near Quincy in the Boston area of Massachusetts. His father, John Adams, who began his working life as a farmer and attorney, went on to become a politician and diplomat. He played a leading role in the American struggle for independence and was a signatory of the Declaration of Independence. John Adams became the second President of the United States, following George Washington, and is an important figure in American history. John Quincy had an older sister, Abigail, and two younger brothers, Thomas and Charles.

In 1777, when John Quincy was 10 years old, he accompanied his father to Europe when he was appointed diplomatic envoy to the French court. The relationship between the Adams's homeland and France at this time was significant: France was supporting the American colony in its developing struggle against British rule. In Paris, John Adams joined Benjamin Franklin, the American ambassador.

There was a brief return home in November 1779 and then John Adams returned to France accompanied by John Quincy and his brother Charles,

The Adams family home in Quincy, Massachusetts, built in 1731 and occupied from 1778 by four generations of the family including John Quincy Adams.

who was two years younger. John Adams enrolled the two boys at a school in Passy outside Paris, where they stayed during the week. He is said to have told John Quincy not to waste too much time on subjects such as geography and arithmetic, and told his masters not to bother with fencing or dancing. The boy was to concentrate on Latin, French and Greek.

After a period of difficult diplomacy, as the war between America and Britain intensified, John Adams was appointed ambassador to the Netherlands and moved with his sons to Amsterdam. In 1781, John Quincy enrolled at the University of Leyden, aged only 14. A few months later, however, he was offered the opportunity to accompany the American envoy to the Court of Catherine the Second of Russia, as his secretary. John Quincy Adams's diplomatic career had begun.

After returning from Russia, John Quincy accompanied his father back to Paris, and on 3 September 1783 the treaty ending the war with Great Britain was signed. Almost immediately, John Adams joined the diplomatic mission to London, taking his son with him. They were soon joined by John Quincy's mother and sister, whom he had scarcely seen since he was 10 years old. They parted again shortly afterwards when John Quincy returned alone to the newly independent United States to attend Harvard University to study law.

Diplomatic life and marriage

John Quincy completed his legal studies and opened a law office in Boston in 1790. Apparently, however, he did not take happily to the law. A breakthrough in his career came in 1794 when President Washington appointed him as minister to the Hague and, accompanied by his younger brother Thomas, he set off again for Europe. His father was by now Vice President and two years later, in 1796, was elected the second President of the United States.

John Quincy met his future wife, Louisa Catherine Johnson, in London in 1794. The daughter of an American merchant from Maryland and his English

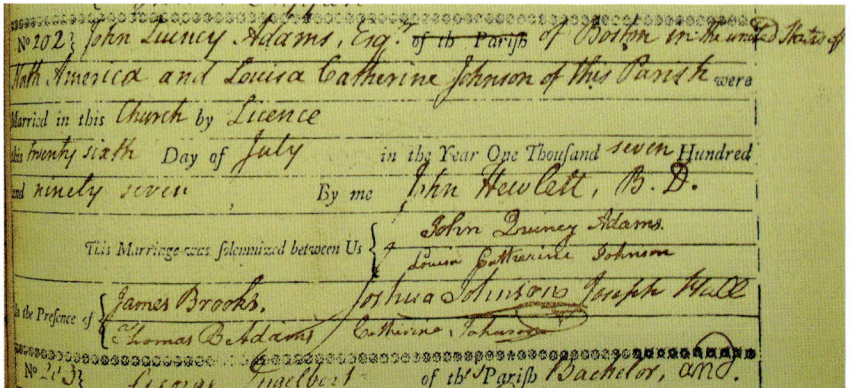

wife, Louisa had lived most of her life in England (although she and John Quincy had originally met as children in Nantes, when she was 4 and he was 12). She was described at the time as an *'attractive, bright and refined young woman, talented musically'* (Ferling, 1996). The couple married in London in 1797 at the church of All Hallows by the Tower, where their entry in the marriage register may still be viewed.

John Quincy went on to undertake diplomatic duties in Berlin, and his reports helped in shaping his father's presidential foreign policy. In 1801, the couple returned to America where Louisa met John Quincy's parents for the first time. By then they had a 6-month-old son, named George Washington Adams, and went on to have two more sons, John and Charles.

John Quincy returned to his legal business and began to play an active role in the political scene, although he was never an enthusiast for party politics. He was elected to the Massachusetts State Legislature and subsequently, in 1803, to the United States Senate. But he did not stay at home for long: in 1809 he was offered the post of minister to Russia, a country already familiar to him. He sailed again for Europe that summer. He was to witness Napoleon's invasion of Russia in 1812.

War and peace

In 1812, war between America and Great Britain was looming again. Confronting Napoleon in Europe, Great Britain was seeking to restrict trade with France, which brought it into conflict with America over shipping. American ships were seized and scuttled. In consequence, America declared war on Great Britain on 18 June 1812. Britain blockaded American ports and there was a sporadic land war between America and Canada. In August 1814 a British force attacked Washington, burning down most of the public buildings.

When peace negotiations were started at Ghent in Belgium, John Quincy Adams was chosen as one of the commissioners. The war was causing great hardship in Britain and when the Duke of Wellington took over as Commander in Chief he entered into negotiations to end it. The peace treaty was signed on Christmas Eve 1814. A few months later, Adams and his family arrived in London, following his appointment as the US minister. Their time here is the subject of this book.

British–American relations in 1815

When the Anglo-American War of 1812 ended with the Treaty of Ghent in 1814, there remained some unresolved issues, mostly about boundaries. For Britain the main concern was the border with Canada and the defence of colonial lands. On the other hand, Britain was America's best customer and the cotton trade was the dominant feature of the economy of both countries. Culturally they also had much in common, with Britain providing plenty of immigrants to America. There were close cultural and religious ties, particularly between non-conformist protestant churches in Britain and their American counterparts.

Chapter 2

The man, his character and family life

John Quincy Adams set up home in August 1815 at Little Boston House in Ealing with his wife Louisa and their three sons, George aged 14, John aged 12 and Charles aged 8. In many ways, the two years the family spent here provided an interlude of unusually close family life. Adams and Louisa had spent much of their married life living away from home in the various European countries where he served as a diplomat. They spent long periods apart from their two elder sons, who were left in the care of relatives at home in Quincy, Massachusetts. Adams, Louisa and Charles arrived in Britain from St Petersburg and were met in London by George and John who had travelled from America. Not having seen George for nearly six years, his parents scarcely recognised him.

Adams and Louisa appear to have enjoyed a close and supportive relationship. Louisa certainly made sacrifices in order to be with her husband. She endured the difficulties and hardships of long sea voyages, overland travel without her husband's support, and life in alien lands, as well as separation from her children. Their fourth child, a daughter, had died in Russia at the age of one.

LRM

Adams, the man

Adams set the highest standards of achievement and personal behaviour for himself and his children, which he, and they, sometimes struggled to meet. The following incident illustrates this:

My brother had remitted to me a Bill of Exchange … payable in London. The bill was accepted 28 February payable by Joseph Denison and Co., no. 106

Fenchurch Street, … and payable this day. I took it to Denisons and there was again referred to Hoare and Barnett Bankers, no. 62 Lombard Street. Of all the insolence I ever experienced there is nothing equal to the insolence of counting house clerks. One of these fellows treated me with so much impertinence, refusing to pay me in the description of bills that I wanted, and telling me in a tone of superciliousness that I must go to the bank, I lost my temper. In his … pomposity he had paid me two pounds ten short of my bill. I threw his papers back in his face, and told him to give me my bill again. He refused; and was attempting to force back upon me the bills I had refused, when a person, apparently a partner of the house or a superior clerk, took them back and gave me the bills I had asked for. I obtained my object, but left the place mortified, and vexed with myself at having been irritated to intemperance by a banker's clerk. (2 May 1817)

The period in Ealing offered Adams an opportunity to become more closely involved in his children's education, particularly that of the eldest, George. He was concerned that George was not nearly well enough prepared to enter Harvard and took him in hand. He writes of a typical day:

I rise with sufficient regularity between five and half-past six o'clock. Rouse my son George, and hear him read five chapters in the French bible; I hold the Latin bible to compare them while he reads; and then read one chapter of the French to him while he holds the Latin. The object is to improve his knowledge and pronunciation of the language. (August 1815 summary)

The rest of the day is taken up with correspondence, visitors, reading newspapers and '*two or three times a week*' travelling into London for business. On other days Adams '*walked with George for an hour and a half before dinner*'.

Adams was clearly highly intelligent, with wide-ranging interests in science, astronomy, literature, history and the social and political questions of the day. He took a close interest in religion and appears to have had strong, if somewhat unorthodox, religious convictions. He had travelled widely, spoke French fluently, and had played a part in many of his country's diplomatic negotiations. His diaries reflect his interests and opinions but say little explicitly about his personal feelings and relationships. However these, and his personality in general, can often be glimpsed through his remarks. Adams comes across as an overachiever burdened with self-doubt. He constantly berates himself in his diary for wasting time and failing to achieve enough.

An outsider, he comments with interest on many aspects of Ealing life. While the family quickly became integrated into the life of the local gentry and professional class, there are indications that Adams would have welcomed inclusion in the higher echelons of society, which he had probably enjoyed in other European countries. Adams describes attending a party hosted by the Lord Mayor at the Mansion House on 8 August 1816. Present were the Duke of Kent (a son of George III and an Ealing resident), the Duke of Wellington and various members of the aristocracy. Adams had been uncertain whether to wear full court or frock dress. He chose the latter, and was rather uncomfortable when most of the company appeared in full court dress:

The Duke of Wellington, 1814. (Thomas Lawrence)

Dined at the Mansion House with the Lord Mayor. It was a dinner to the Duke of Wellington, and for the purpose of presenting to him a resolution of thanks from the Common Council of London voted shortly after the Battle of Waterloo, and upon that occasion. The party was small. A single table of about thirty-six persons. … I was the only foreign minister present; a favour for which I have more than once been indebted to the present Lord Mayor; without precisely knowing why. Probably because he is a Whig; and friendly to liberal principles with regard to America. I had been doubtful whether to go in full Court Dress to this party, or in Frock Dress. On consulting Mr Bourke, he advised me to go in Frock. I accordingly went so but found the Lord Mayor and most of the Company in Full Dress. The Duke of Kent, however, the only person of the Royal family who attended, came in Frock – as did the Earl of Darnley and his son Lord Clifton. The Duke of Wellington himself and his aids de Camp, Lord Arthur Hill, and Colonels Percy, Harvey and Freemantle, were in military uniform. Lord Erskine and the Aldermen were in Court dress. I apologised for being in Undress. Before dinner the Lord Mayor introduced me to the Duke of Wellington. I observed that I had already been introduced to him – Oh! yes! said he – at Paris – no – at the Prince Regent's last levee at Carlton House, by your Grace's brother, Mr Wellesley Pole – Oh! Aye! Yes! said the Duke, who had obviously forgotten me and my introduction. This is one of many incidents from which I can perceive how very small a space my person or my station occupy in the notice of those persons and at these places. (8 August 1816)

A couple of days later Adams is worrying about wasting time. He writes:

The dissipation of one day abroad produces as usual the dissipation of the next day at home. Not positive idleness but an incapacity for steady application, which wastes the time in trifling. Having moved in crab-like fashion, upon my Diary index, backwards through the months of June, May and April, I made this morning a start back to the first of January of the present year. (10 August 1816)

Family life

It was not all work, and there are plenty of references to leisure, walks and family activities. Local walks, with one or more members of the family, were taken more or less daily. This passage illustrates a typical Sunday's activities as well as Adams's interests in both religion and cosmology:

George's reading, and half a page again of this journal, occupied me this morning until breakfast time. We all went to church and heard the whole service performed for Advent Sunday by Mr Lewis. His sermon was from Luke Ch.X.v.37 upon the story of the Good Samaritan. I believe it is impossible to make a bad sermon upon that subject. … Mr Lewis is a very indifferent preacher, but there is much inequality in his discourses, and this was one of his best. After church I walked from Ealing to Gunnersbury and through Brentford home. … The evening was clear and cold, and I was looking for the new moon. (3 December 1815)

On 20 August 1816 Adams walked all the way home from his office in Central London (a distance of about 8 miles), arriving at 7.15 pm. He found Ellen Nicholas, daughter of Dr George Nicholas, headmaster of Great Ealing School, and other ladies there. The party continued until 11 pm, with Miss Nicholas playing the piano and singing. Dinners and social engagements within a circle of local families took place frequently and Adams, for all his anxiety about wasting time, appears to have enjoyed them.

Another side to Adams's nature is also perhaps unwittingly revealed in his diary. Ellen Nicholas became a close companion of his wife Louisa, but it also seems possible that Adams was attracted to the young woman. In October 1816, in response to verses she had written, he was writing poetry to her – as described in Chapter 5.

When in London, in1815, both Louisa and Adams had their portraits painted by the celebrated artist C. R. Leslie.

Adams never reveals in his diary anything about his personal feelings for his wife, whom he usually refers to as 'Mrs Adams'. His references to her are generally factual and simply record her domestic and social activities. Louisa must have been continuously occupied in managing the household and servants, visiting and receiving visitors, nursing the sick (including Adams himself as illustrated in Chapter 11) and helping Adams with such tasks as writing letters. She also found time for fishing on the Grand Union (formerly Grand Junction) Canal, which seems to have been one of her favourite pastimes, with a number of outings in August 1816:

Walk to Ealing across the fields and to Hanwell. Mrs Adams and George after he returned from school went to fish until dinner time. (6 August 1816)

Mrs Adams went and fished upon the Grand Junction Canal. I walked on the tow-path along by its side to the cross lane from Sion House to the Uxbridge Road; and returned by the way of Hanwell. I was not before acquainted with this walk. There were two boats returning to the Stourbridge iron works by this canal, a distance of 185 miles, which one of the boatmen told me they travelled in five days. (19 August 1816)

A modern-day view of the Grand Union Canal near Brentford.

The Grand Junction Canal

At the time of Adams's arrival in London in 1815, canals were a relatively recent innovation in the London area. The Grand Junction Canal (renamed the Grand Union in 1929), which connects London (at Brentford) with Birmingham, was built during the 1790s – starting from both ends.

The stretch of canal which Adams refers to several times, usually in connection with his wife and children fishing on it, would presumably have been the section just to the west of his home, running from Brentford, where the canal meets the Thames, north-west towards Osterley and Hanwell.

Britain has the oldest national canal system in the world, with its first arm – the Bridgewater Canal – opening between Worsley and Manchester in 1761. Created in the decades before the railways, they enabled faster and more reliable transfer of the materials that fuelled the industrial revolution. By the time of its completion, the network had about 1800 miles of canals. Today, this network is used mostly for leisure, and the part used by Adams and his family can still be followed by walking, cycling or boating.

The section includes the noted Hanwell Flight of Locks, a sequence of six closely spaced locks created in 1794, which raises the water level by over 50 feet within a half-mile stretch. Each lock was built to accommodate one 14-foot-wide barge or two 7-foot-wide narrow boats side by side. This engineering masterpiece is now a scheduled Ancient Monument.

Adams was sometimes drawn into domestic concerns, as when in November 1815 there was trouble with the servants and an attempted burglary:

While I was in town yesterday there was a great stir and hubbub among the female servants of the house, against whom Mrs Adams had received strong and well founded complaints. They had no defence against the charges and could only resort to mutual criminations about one another. Mrs Adams gave notice to three of them: Mrs Brooks the cook, Margaret Wedge the housemaid, and Ann Prudden the laundry maid. They are accordingly to quit at the expiration of a month from the day of notice. There was an attempt made last night to break open the house. My son George, Lucy Hanel my wife's chambermaid, and Richard Brant the English footman were all waked by the noise and got up, though lodging in different parts of the house. Richard finally thought it was only a rat between the walls, but Lucy said she heard a whistling. The attempt however happily proved abortive. (23 November 1815)

Throughout the family's time in Ealing, the diaries paint a picture of Adams as a caring husband who relied on his wife's support in managing the domestic sphere and playing her part socially. As for his relationship with his children, we see both over-anxious concern about their progress and fairly close involvement in their upbringing. Given the long periods of time Adams had spent apart from his sons, this opportunity for close family life was unusual, and he may have had a sense of urgency in trying to make up for lost time. In some ways he seems to have been relaxed and tolerant – for example, allowing the boys to attend a dissenting chapel while he and Louisa attend the local Anglican church, St Mary's, in Ealing.

The family were regulars at the many fairs, races and other 'low' entertainments held in the Ealing area at the time (see Chapter 6). There are also many references in the diaries to family outings to local talks and the theatre and to walks. The boys often came home from school bringing friends to stay for dinner. But there is a constant undercurrent of worry, particularly about George. At the end of June 1816, when the three boys come home for the summer holidays, Adams writes of his concern that *'I can neither find nor make leisure to employ their time advantageously for themselves'.* The reading and translation of the Latin and French bibles with George appear to have been a priority and never varied unless George was ill.

At the end of 1815 a passage in the diary illustrates Adams's feelings in a way that is revealing, showing how he valued this interval of family life:

The close of the year is to be noted with fervent gratitude to the Giver of all good gifts, for the favours of all my life and especially of the year. It has been remarkable by my removal to England, and by the reunion of all my family around me. May the blessing of God be granted to the results of both these events!

Chapter 3

Ealing in 1815

The Ealing of 1815 that John Quincy Adams came to know had remained mostly unchanged for many centuries but would be virtually unrecognisable today. The parish of Ealing was relatively large, stretching from the River Brent in the north down to the Thames in the south. It included not only the whole of the present-day town of Ealing, but also the eastern part of modern Brentford known as Old Brentford. These areas are now suburbs of Greater London.

The parish population was about 6,000 (compared with about 100,000 today), a large proportion of which was concentrated in the busy industrial community of Old Brentford. The remainder of the parish was rural in character, with the population centred around the parish church of St Mary's in the village known as Ealing Town or Great Ealing and in the outlying hamlets of Little Ealing, Ealing Haven (now Ealing Broadway), Ealing Dean (now West Ealing) and Drayton Green.

The contrast between the quiet village of Ealing and the bustling riverside town of Brentford was very marked. The wide-ranging industries along Brentford High Street and the river included a malt distillery, a soap factory, a tile kiln and a brewery. By 1800 the arrival of the Grand Junction Canal had led to Brentford becoming a busy Thames junction for water transport carrying goods to and from the Midlands.

Although the railways did not arrive in Ealing for another 20 years, the area was nevertheless well served for transport into London and out to the west. From his home in Little Ealing, Adams's usual route into London was along the Bath Road, which ran through Brentford High Street and on into the city via Chiswick and Kensington. This was an important coaching road with numerous inns to service the trade – along the route through Brentford there were an estimated 30 inns.

Ealing, on the other hand, had 14 inns, many of which were along another major coaching road, the Uxbridge Road, which led out to Oxford and beyond. Many of these are still public houses today. In the old Ealing Town, there was the New Inn, almost opposite St Mary's Church, from where Thomas Ives's local coach service journeyed into London at 8.30 am, 1.30 pm and 3 pm. These coaches also carried the post to and from Ealing, which was collected at the general shop of J. Blake. The New Inn, with its adjacent hall, was a focal point of community life and Adams would visit it on many occasions. It stood on the site of the present public house of the same name, although today's New Inn is a different building. Curiously, Adams makes no mention of the Plough public house in Little Ealing, even though it was his nearest inn and is probably Ealing's oldest.

The principal focal point for the community, and indeed for Adams, was the parish church of St Mary's. The medieval church had been replaced in the

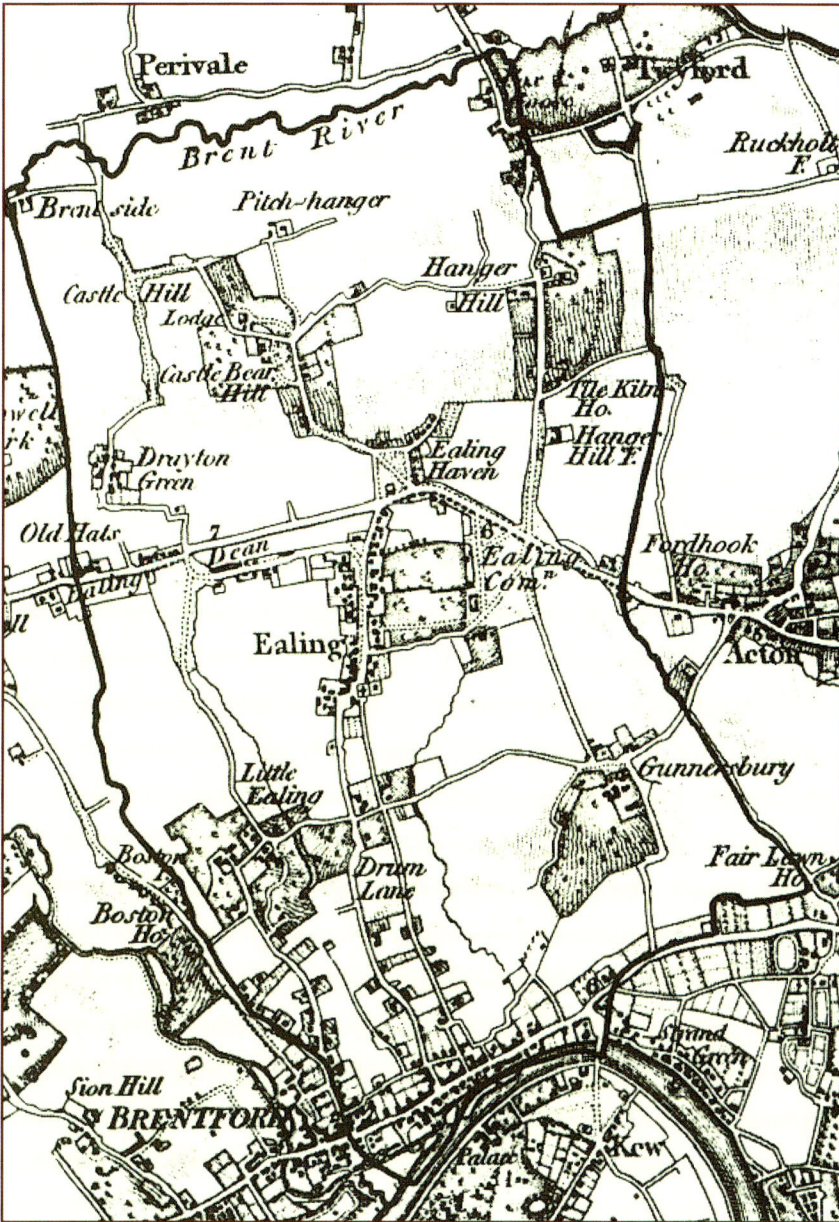

Ealing in 1822.

1730s by what was described at the time as a *'modest red-brick box'*, a typically Georgian building: plain and rectangular with a small tower. This structure remains today, albeit in unrecognisable form, as the core of the Victorian neo-Gothic conversion of the 1860s. There were well-established lanes and footpaths leading to the church from all parts of the parish.

Parish affairs were controlled by the Vestry, which was chaired by the vicar, the Reverend Dr Colston Carr, and made up of churchwardens and overseers. In most respects, the Vestry had a similar function to today's local council.

St Mary's Church, c. 1800.

It levied rates for a variety of purposes, among the most important of which were the maintenance of the roads and provision for the poor. The village poor house was to close in 1839, but its buildings, now private houses, still stand today opposite the church at 72 and 74 St Mary's Road.

Eminent residents

In the early nineteenth century Ealing was noted for its many handsome residences and, judging by the number of eminent residents, this could almost be regarded as Ealing's golden age. The parish rate books for that year record as residents a duke, two generals and an admiral, as well as many distinguished gentlemen. In 1810, Sir John Soane, one of the country's leading architects, had sold his country home at Pitzhanger Manor on Ealing Green. Soane had redesigned the house in his own original style and was using it largely as a 'show house' for potential clients.

Lady Jane Carr

In 1812, Prime Minister and Ealing resident Spencer Perceval was assassinated in the House of Commons. His widow Jane and 12 children continued to live at Elm Grove, a large mansion on the south side of Ealing Common. In early 1815, Jane Perceval, then in her mid-40s, remarried to a Colonel Sir Henry Carr. When Adams attends church for the first time he notes in his diary:

The church service was read by an old clergyman, Dr Carr, the father of Col. Carr who married Mrs Perceval. (6 August 1815)

Adams, as a politician himself, seems very conscious that the widow of the last prime minister lived in the neighbourhood:

Col. Sir Henry Carr is the person whom the widow of the late Prime Minister, Mr Perceval, married to the great surprise of the public. They reside at Ealing but have a house also in town. (15 December 1815)

Adams notes the presence of Colonel Carr at various social gatherings in Ealing that he attends, but does not report conversing with him. The diaries also indicate that he was genuinely disappointed not to have met Lady Carr. At a cricket match at Gunnersbury Park, Adams records all those present. Many eminent Ealing residents attended, but he notes that neither Lady Carr nor any of her family were there.

The Duke of Kent

Probably the most well known resident living in Ealing at this time was Prince Edward, Duke of Kent (1767–1820), the fourth son of George III. Unlike the nearby riverside villages of Kew and Richmond, Ealing did not have significant associations with royalty, and the Duke residing in Ealing was doubtless a matter of some local pride. The Duke finally married in 1818 at the age of 50, the marriage ceremony being held at Kew Palace, and the following year he fathered a daughter who would become Queen Victoria.

Within the first few weeks of arriving in Ealing, Adams records:

We all went to church, and heard a charity sermon, preached by a Dr Crane before the Duke of Kent, for the benefit of the Charity School in the Parish of Ealing. (20 August 1815)

The Percevals and the Walpoles

Lady Carr's marriage to Colonel Carr was short-lived, as he died in 1821 at the age of only 44. She continued to occupy Elm Grove along with her single daughters until her death in 1844. The Percevals remained very much an Ealing family. One of the daughters, Isabel, married Spencer Walpole MP, who would later be Home Secretary, and lived at a house called The Hall on Ealing Green, next door to Pitzhanger Manor which Walpole then also owned. Upon the death of Jane Carr it was arranged that the four remaining single Perceval daughters would occupy Pitzhanger Manor. Here 'the ladies of the manor house' became a well-known feature of Victorian Ealing, all living well into old age. The youngest, Frederica, was the last to die, in 1901, at the age of 94. She was the last resident of Pitzhanger Manor before it became a public library the following year. All four unmarried daughters are buried in a single tomb in South Ealing Cemetery.

Pitzhanger Manor, 1804, as rebuilt by Sir John Soane shortly before Adams arrived in Ealing.

It seems that curiosity may have got the better of Adams:

After church we took a ride over Castlebar Hill, where the Duke of Kent resides, and on returning I alighted with George and walked home. (20 August 1815)

The residence was Castle Hill Lodge, which Edward had bought in 1801 from Maria Fitzherbert, the morganatic wife of his brother George, who was the eldest son of George III and who would become George IV. Edward had the house rebuilt and refurbished at considerable expense. A contemporary report described it:

The building is of rather low but of pleasing proportions. The chief front stands towards the north, and has in the centre a portico, with four Ionic columns, surmounted by a triangular pediment, the tympanum being vacant. The hill on

which the structure is placed descends from this front with a gentle sweep, and a prospect of some extent is obtained over a tract of country which is of an agreeable though not of an eminently picturesque character. (Brewer, 1816)

The presence of the Duke in Ealing is noted on many occasions by Adams. For example:

On my way home the Duke of Kent, driving a phaeton with Madame de Saint Laurent, passed by me, returning to his house at Castlebar Hill. (3 August 1816)

The exotically named Madame de Saint Laurent was the Duke's long-term French mistress, who lived with him in considerable style at Castle Hill Lodge. Adams also met the Duke on many formal occasions in London and, in particular, at functions hosted by the Lord Mayor at the Mansion House, where the Duke was often required to speak on behalf of the King and the royal family. Adams's dealings with the Duke of Kent were largely on a formal basis and the Duke always seemed polite and affable towards him.

The Duke of Kent's younger brother, Prince Augustus, Duke of Sussex, in contrast to his older brother, displayed a rather irreverent attitude to his position in the royal family, even expressing some sympathies with republicanism. His liberal views found an understanding audience in Adams and the pair became friends, with the Duke of Sussex actually visiting the Adams home at Little Boston for dinner on one occasion.

In the diaries, the Duke of Kent comes across as a conscientious and hard-working member of the royal family, who was the patron of many charities both locally and nationally. However, at the time, the Duke had the reputation of being a spendthrift, perhaps exemplified by the fact that, somewhat unusually, he had his own band, which often played at public or charitable events.

23

Adams's contacts with the Duke of Kent proved to be short lived, as the Duke soon removed himself to Brussels. Oblique reference is made in the diaries to this situation when, in September 1816, General Sir Frederick Wetherall (1754–1840) visits Little Boston enquiring about a former servant of Adams's, Peter Pio:

General Wetherall immediately afterwards called on me to enquire from the Duke of Kent Peter Pio's character. Pio is at Bruxelles and is endeavouring to enter the Duke of Kent's service. I gave the General as good a character of Pio as I could consistently with truth and candour. … The General is Comptroller of the Duke of Kent's household and lives near the Duke's seat at Castlebar

The Kentish Lottery

Adams was obviously not aware of the circumstances or the reason for the Duke of Kent's departure to Brussels. Like many of the sons of George III, the Duke of Kent lived well beyond his means and by 1815 the financers of the well-appointed Castle Hill Lodge were seeking further security from the Duke. The Duke's response was quietly to leave the country.

After the birth of Princess Victoria in 1819 the Duke found himself back in favour and a request was made to Parliament that the house be sold by lottery. This rather ill-judged suggestion occasioned a well-known satirical cartoon of the time called 'The Kentish Lottery'. After numerous attempts to sell the house the loyal General Wetherall bought it himself in 1829. Castle Hill Lodge was demolished in about 1845 and replaced by the house on Castlebar Road that is now St David's Home for Disabled Servicemen.

The Kentish Lottery cartoon.

Hill, which he invited me to go and see. He says the Duke who has now fixed his residence for some years at Bruxelles will come to England for a few days next month. (18 September 1816)

General Wetherall had a distinguished military career serving his country all over the world. He had been the Duke of Kent's aide-de-camp in Canada and the West Indies and had rejoined the Duke in Ealing in 1815 as his equerry, living nearby at Castlebar House (a little further down Castlebar Hill from the Duke's residence). He was a godfather of Queen Victoria and later an executor of the Duke of Kent's will – a task that was to prove particularly irksome.

General Dumouriez

Adams was no doubt intrigued to discover that the infamous General Dumouriez lived near him in Little Ealing. Charles Dumouriez (1739–1823) was an exiled French general who resided at Rochester House in Little Ealing from 1812 to 1822. This house still exists at the junction of Northfield Avenue and Little Ealing Lane. He had a distinguished military career prior to the French Revolution and thereafter played a leading role in the revolutionary government. However, he became heavily embroiled in the political machinations following the restoration of the monarchy and was forced into exile, ending up in England in 1804. Here, he was able to negotiate terms with the British government and supplied intelligence to them on the political situation in France.

Adams took an early opportunity to meet with Dumouriez, and noted:

I paid a visit to General Dumouriez, who is almost my next door neighbour, and returned to him the letters which were left with me about a fortnight since, with several letters from the Post Office. The letters had given me some insight into the views and present situation of the man, and I had now a long conversation with him which gave me more. Dumouriez was at one time an important personage in the world. It is now more than twenty years since he was obliged to fly from the army which he had led to victory, and seek refuge among the enemies whom he had vanquished. He is now seventy five years of age, burning with ambition to return to France. (26 August 1815)

Adams conversed with Dumouriez in French and found what he had to say about the situation in France very interesting, faithfully recording everything he said. At the same time he found his manner and opinions tiresome:

The ineradicable vices of his character are Vanity, Levity and Insincerity. They are conspicuous in his writings and were not less remarkable in his conversation with me. Like all vain people his greatest delight is to talk of himself. (26 August 1815)

Dumouriez explained to Adams the circumstances of his coming to Britain and how he lived:

He told me that he had been twelve years in the service of this country. That he had first been sent for, to assist in a plan of defence for this country against a French invasion. He had made his bargain with the British Government. They had offered him terms which he had accepted, and he lived upon them

Rochester House in the eighteenth century and its most famous resident, General Dumouriez.

comfortably, though not in opulence. … He was here upon good terms with all parties; the ministers and opposition were all his friends. He gave his opinions freely, as he thought might be useful, and wrote memoirs when required. He had resided in his present habitation these two years and a half, with the Count de St Martin his Aid de Camp and his wife. They had lost their only son, in Portugal. He saw very little society here, and very seldom went to London. (26 August 1815)

On many occasions, Dumouriez praises his former associate Prince Louis Philippe, the Duke of Orleans (1773–1850), who himself was in exile and living nearby in Twickenham. The Duke would in later years return to France as king. Many history books refer to Louis Philippe as having an association with Ealing, in that at some stage he taught at Great Ealing School. Adams, however, makes no reference to this in his diaries, despite his sons attending that school. Dumouriez regularly met with Louis Philippe – perhaps plotting their eventual return to France.

The descriptions of Dumouriez in the diaries paint a very full picture of the General's character. On one occasion he gives Adams his unsolicited views on the United States, the dispute with the Creek Indians, the difficulties of relations with Canada and New Mexico, and the likelihood of another war with Britain. Adams comments:

On all these subjects he had some information; but it was all partial, and such as he had apparently imbibed from those with whom he converses concerning them here. In combating his prejudices, I did not expect to alter his opinions;

nor would it that I know, have been of any use if it had. (10 October 1815)

Considering that Adams was the representative of a foreign government, Dumouriez seemed to be remarkably indiscreet in what he disclosed to Adams:

He passed to the subject of France, where he said everything was dark and gloomy. He read me an extract of a letter which he said he had just received, and which was from the Government there. … The General read to me also a letter from the Duke of Wellington which he received a few days since – dated the 26th of September, and he gave me the copy of his answer to it dated 4th October. (10 October 1815)

As the months passed, Adams and Dumouriez met less frequently. It seems the General became increasingly resigned to the fact that he might never return to France, although he still took great satisfaction from being a close confidant of the Duke of Orleans. Adams notes:

He appears to have abandoned his expectations of being recalled to take upon him the administration of affairs in France, and he disapproves of what has been done and is doing there. … He spoke in the highest terms of the Duke of Orleans, who he said was a 'parfaitement honnête homme', of whom he boasted he now saw every week. The Duke he said sometimes came to see him, and sometimes sent his carriage for him. (30 January 1816)

Dumouriez is portrayed by Adams as an eccentric old man with a declining influence in both France and Britain, still living on past glories, and with a decreasing social circle. When Adams comes to leave Ealing, Dumouriez seems genuinely sad to see him go:

I had some conversation with Dumouriez, who is more cautious in talking about French affairs than heretofore. He lamented the absence of his friend the Duke of Kent, who he said would reside abroad at least two years longer. And now his other friend the Duke of Orleans was also gone, and he told me all the particulars of the Duke's return. … The old General came out with me to his gate and bade me farewell with a compliment in the French style. (27 April 1817)

Chapter 4

Little Boston House

When the Adams family arrived in London at the end of May 1815 they took up temporary accommodation at 67 Harley Street in Marylebone, central London. From here, Adams busied himself with setting up his office in Craven Street (near present-day Charing Cross Station) and all the necessary formal introductions as American minister. Meanwhile, Louisa had responsibility for finding permanent accommodation. Adams reports in his diary:

My wife went out of town seven miles to look at a house to be let for the summer. (21 July 1815)

I have engaged a house called Little Boston House at Ealing, seven miles from London from the first of August until the first of January, and we are to go out there next Tuesday, but for the convenience of Americans who may have occasion to apply for passports particularly, or for other business, I think it necessary to have an office in town. (28 July 1815)

For an American minister to choose an out-of-town residence as his home was rather unusual. Obviously there were financial savings, but it appears that Adams was more concerned with his sons' future education and felt that, in order for them to dedicate themselves to study, they should be removed from the hurly-burly and distractions of the metropolis.

According to the parish rate books, there had been a house on the site of Little Boston House since at least 1700. In 1796, a Gabriel Matthias had rebuilt the house to make it:

a compleat dwelling for a private Man and his family as I make six bed chambers besides servants. It has cost me a great deal of money. (private correspondence, 21 April 1796)

The house fronted onto Windmill Lane (now Windmill Road) on the corner of a lane now known as 'The Ride', which led to Boston Manor House. Little Boston House was part of the estate of Boston Manor, which had been owned by a family of wealthy City merchants, the Clitherows,

since 1670. When Adams arrived, the lord of Boston Manor was the fourth James Clitherow (1766–1841). The Boston Manor estate was immediately to the east of the River Brent in the area known as New Brentford, then in the parish of Hanwell. In 1805, shortly after becoming lord of the manor, Clitherow had bought extensive lands in the Little Ealing area, which had included Little Boston House. It is probable that the house then became known as 'Little Boston', replacing the name 'Nightingale Hall' which Adams sometimes refers to in the diaries as being an alternative name.

It seems likely that the Clitherow family intended to use Little Boston

Boston Manor estate

Much of the land to the south west of Little Ealing was part of the Boston Manor estate, owned by the Clitherow family. Boston Manor House dates from 1623. The third James Clitherow seems to have taken a keen interest in plants, and planted the cedar trees that still dominate the park around the house. The Grand Junction (now Grand Union) Canal was built through the grounds in 1794. The fourth James Clitherow and his wife Jane were very active in local good causes and charity work. This brought them into association with the Duke of Clarence (the future King William IV) and his wife Adelaide, and they were personally invited to his coronation. The royal couple dined at the house in 1834.

House as a dower house. At the time of the Adams's tenancy the owners were Mary Clitherow and Lady Martha Seymour, the sisters of the fourth James Clitherow. From the diaries it appears that Adams did not have much to do with the Clitherow family; communication was largely by correspondence with Mary Clitherow and concerned the terms of the tenancy. This was conducted in a formal but cordial manner. The Clitherow sisters clearly had no need to occupy the property themselves and were pleased to be quite flexible about the length of the tenancy.

The Adams family found Little Boston House very suitable for their purposes and in time became very fond of it:

The house which we have taken is not large, but neat and elegant, and fitted up with all that minute attention to comfort which is characteristic of English domestic life. We have a coach house and stable, dairy, fruit and kitchen garden. (2 August 1815)

The grounds were of some two acres and stretched back alongside the Ride towards Boston Manor House. The Adams family found these grounds very pleasant, often walking in them after dinner. In the summer of 1816,

The Colonel's Drive, now The Ride, leading up to Boston Manor House, c. 1906. Little Boston House is immediately to the right.

THE COLONELS DRIVE BRENTFORD.

Boston Manor House, 1796.

Adams becomes positively poetic when describing the gardens:

The season has been backward, almost beyond example. There has been yet scarcely a day of warm weather; but the face of the country has been exquisitely beautiful. Our garden though small, is laid out with taste and elegance, with forest trees, fruit trees, shrubs, plants, herbs, kitchen vegetables and flowers in profusion. It is a little paradise, vocal with the harmony of every feathered songster of the spring. (30 June 1816)

Little Boston after Adams

After the Adams family departed in 1817, Little Boston House continued to be owned by the Clitherow family until shortly before its demolition in about 1930. During this period it was rented out as a family house and, unusually, had two more notable residents.

In 1874 General Adam Badeau, United States Consul General, is recorded as having lived at the house. General Badeau had a distinguished record in the American Civil War serving under General Grant and then holding several overseas diplomatic posts including Madrid and Havana, as well as London. His occupancy suggests that the Clitherow family may have maintained some association with the American Government.

From 1916 to 1925 Little

A view of the rear of Little Boston House in the 1920s.

Boston was the home of the curiously named actor Eille Norwood. He played Sherlock Holmes in 47 films between 1921 and 1923, appearing on screen as the detective more than any other actor. He was noted for his adeptness at disguises and was said to be a particular favourite of Conan Doyle.

Charles Adams, John Quincy's youngest son, later served as the American minister to Britain (1861–1868), and visited his childhood home while in London.

The 1920s and 30s saw the sale of many landed estates in the area for building development. Boston Manor was no exception and as part of the break-up of the estate the Little Boston property was sold in 1925 to Charles Jackman, a local builder and later mayor of Ealing, who moved into the house with his family. While living in the house he began to build the houses now numbered 236 to 260 Windmill Road and in about 1930 Little Boston was demolished. The only remnant is the old boundary wall alongside the Ride, and number 236 is to this day called 'Little Boston'.

Joan Bellefeuille sitting in the garden of Little Boston House, c. 1927.

Memories of Little Boston

Joan Bellefeuille, a daughter of Charles Jackman, wrote to the Little Ealing History Group in 2003 from Canada, where she lived until her death in 2010. She had childhood memories of the original Little Boston House:

My memories are those of a child living there. The house had three floors and a basement. The top floor was like an attic and was used as servants' quarters. The second floor had many bedrooms and one very large room, which was the ballroom with large windows each of which had a small iron balcony overlooking the garden. Downstairs there was a living room, dining room, morning room and drawing room. The large kitchen was in the basement, also a good-sized wine cellar. The kitchen had a big old black stove, large cupboards and an old granite sink with a wooden plate rack over it.

The grounds around the house were quite extensive, stretching from The Ride along Windmill Road to the sports field and going down The Ride to Boston Manor Road. To one side of the house was a cottage and a carriage house, probably for a groom and gardener. At the back of the house was a large conservatory which produced a beautiful white rose every Christmas. The rest of the garden was much neglected and overgrown but there were the remains of a walled garden used for growing vegetables and fruit. It was fascinating because the fruit trees had been trained with their branches tied to the wall so that the sun could heat the brick and so hasten the ripening of the fruit. In this way even peaches were grown. There were many trees in the garden; one cedar of note was reputed to be 500 years old.

Chapter 5

Ealing society

A dams was an intellectually inquisitive and gregarious man who enjoyed conversation. By the same token there was a natural curiosity on the part of people in Ealing when they discovered they had the American minister in their midst. As a consequence, Adams and his family rapidly became part of Ealing society. At the outset, friendships were formed through the parish church and the boys' school.

Dr George Nicholas

Adams quickly became friends with Dr George Nicholas (1763–1829), the headmaster of Great Ealing

Louisa was an accomplished musician who often contributed to after-dinner musical entertainment. (Charles Bird King)

School, which his sons attended, and the two families grew very close. Within a month Adams had been invited to dine at Dr Nicholas's home:

We all dined at Doctor Nicholas's. The company at dinner consisted of the Dr's eldest daughter and two eldest sons, and several ladies and gentlemen of the neighbourhood – Mrs Wims, the wife of a general of that name, with a Miss Blair, Mr and Mrs Copland, Mr and Mrs Morrison and Mr and Mrs Gray, and a Mr Von Harten, a German. … Our entertainment was the most elegant and sumptuous of any that I have been at in England. After dinner the ladies retired, and the gentlemen sat upwards of an hour longer. On returning to the parlour we found there Dr Nicholas's three younger daughters. There were cards and one whist party was made. Mrs Copland and the eldest Miss Nicholas played upon the piano and the harp and sang very well. Dr Nicholas's two sons had been shooting partridges from four o'clock this morning. The season for shooting commences this day. Mr Copland told me he was going on a shooting party down into Norfolk. It was between 11 and 12 o'clock when we came home.
(1 September 1815)

Adams and Dr Nicholas were of a similar age and shared outlooks and interests. On one occasion the reported conversation seems to amount to little more than gossip:

In my walk before dinner I went round by the school, called upon the Doctor, and paid the bill. He is going in the course of two or three days for Wales, being detained tomorrow to attend a meeting of a charitable association for the relief of schoolmasters decayed and their widows, of which the Duke of Kent is the Patron. The Duke, he said, had sent him a message with a particular request that he would attend tomorrow. He was very full of conversation, and told me that the Duke of Norfolk, just deceased had left, he heard, eighty-seven natural children. (21 December 1815)

The Nicholas family

Dr George Nicholas was a widower with nine children – four sons and five daughters – all in their twenties and teens, as well as a young ward called Annette Mansell. Louisa Adams and, indeed, Adams himself seemed to actively enjoy the company of young people and all the Nicholas children were regular visitors to Little Boston.

The four Nicholas sons were George Frederick, Francis, Edward and Alfred. George Frederick and Francis (referred to in the diaries as Frank) were later to follow their father as headmasters of Great Ealing School. George Frederick, the eldest, was a student at King's College, Cambridge, and Adams took a particular interest in the nature of his education:

Caroline Nicholas spent the day here, and her brother George dined with us. He had sent a hare and a pair of partridges of his own shooting as a present to Mrs Adams. … George Nicholas is an undergraduate at King's College, Cambridge, and though an undergraduate, is a fellow of the College. I made some enquiries of him respecting the course of his studies there, which are different in every college. They are required to attend four terms every year, for three years and a half. But the terms are so short that they have more than half the year in vacation, and the only exercise that they have to attend is to a tutor once a day to whom they construe Euripides's Tragedies. There are however lectures which it is optional with them to attend or not. The students of King's College are all sent from Eton School and undergo their examinations there. They enjoy many privileges, and after keeping the regular number of terms, demand their degrees … as of right. (4 October 1816)

The five Nicholas daughters were Caroline, Ellen, Laura, Charlotte and Sophia. Ellen, the second eldest, was particularly close to Louisa Adams, often staying at Little Boston when Louisa was ill and accompanying her on trips to London. The motherless Ellen Nicholas may have fulfilled for Louisa the roles of both companion and perhaps the grown-up daughter she never had. Ellen is portrayed in the diaries as an attractive and vivacious young woman, who is an accomplished pianist and singer at the after-dinner entertainments.

As a diversionary pastime, Louisa and Ellen started to write poetry and encouraged Adams to join them. Adams could not resist the challenge:

Finished my verses. Ellen Nicholas wrote a few days ago some complimentary lines to my wife, and both of them have been urging me for some time to write something for them to set to music. I pleaded the barrenness of my imagination as long as I could, but in return for Ellen's poetry, something was become indispensable. In my walk of the day before yesterday, I strained from hard bound brains, two stanzas of eight lines, in the amatory style; and as with a serious turn they would have been ridiculous from me to her, I closed the second stanza with a hyperbolical and burlesque idea. Yesterday morning at breakfast I gave them to her. She was pleased with them and my wife told me I had never written any half so pretty for her. But not being satisfied with them myself, I added several stanzas while riding from Town yesterday, and one this morning to conclude, prepared as I was rising from bed. For I can allow to this trifling only time in which I can do nothing else. But there is an incongruity in the lines, because the additional stanzas, instead of the ludicrous character of the second, are too serious and even solemn, written as if from a youthful and ardent lover, and expressing sentiments which I neither do nor ought to feel for her. The love is all merely poetical, but has so much the appearance of reality, that I scruple to show the lines now they are written. (12 October 1816)

Despite his protestations, we might infer that Adams was attracted to Ellen and expressed this in the form of writing verse to please her.

During the autumn of 1816, Ellen Nicholas stayed at Little Boston with the Adams family for three months while Louisa was ill, and when Ellen finally returned home Adams appeared genuinely to miss her:

Since Ellen Nicholas left us there has been no evening music – I usually pass the evening however from dinner time with my family, sometimes as idly and sometimes reading. (December 1816 summary)

The literary scene

This was a time of the Romantic Movement and exceptional literary development. Among those writing during the period were Wordsworth, Coleridge, Shelley, Byron, Keats, Austen, Blake and Scott. The growing literate middle class had the money to buy books and periodicals and the leisure to read them. Adams refers to reading novels by Maria Edgeworth, a popular writer of the time, and to Byron:

Brought out with me Lord Byron's third Canto of Child Harold, *which I read after dinner. He is perhaps the most fashionable poet of the age, but his poetry is not made I think of lasting materials. The subject of this poem allows him to be as desultory as he pleases. So it treats of himself, his daughter, the battle of Waterloo, Napoleon, Major Howard, Ehrenbreitstein, General Marceau, the Rhine, the Lake of Geneva, Clarens, Rousseau, Gibbon, Voltaire, and a lady in England whom Lord Byron loves, but who is not his wife. The train of thought is original, wild, romantic, and bordering on distraction. The versification singular but habitually reversing the sense from time to time, to the utter discomfiture of Harmony – The sentiment sometimes tender, but always with a mixture of gloom and fierceness. The best stanzas in this Canto are those upon Napoleon.* (10 December 1816)

Memorial to Ellen Nicholas

There is a greater sadness to the story of Ellen Nicholas. Many figures in Ealing society of this period were not buried in the Ealing parish church graveyard, but in the tranquil setting by the banks of the River Brent at St Mary's Church, Perivale. Only two years after Adams was writing his verses to her, Ellen Nicholas was buried there. In the church there is a memorial to her by the eminent sculptor Richard Westmacott.

To the cherished memory of
ELLEN FRANCIS NICHOLAS
Daughter of the Revd. Dr GEORGE
NICHOLAS of Ealing
and his wife ELIZABETH
lovely accomplished most
affectionate and most affectionately
beloved
After a severe struggle of twelve
weeks with a painful illness
she was released from suffering on
the 22nd of October 1818
in the 21st year of her age
leaving her sorrowing relatives no
consolation but the hope of meeting
with her in a better world, never to
part again

Friendship with the Nicholas family led to introductions to a small circle of Ealing families who dined with each other regularly. Among these were Mr Alexander Copland and Major Alexander Morrison who lived in adjacent properties called 'Gunnersbury Park' and 'Gunnersbury House', today known as the 'Large Mansion' and the 'Small Mansion' in the grounds of Gunnersbury Park.

Alexander Copland

Alexander Copland (1774–1834) was a rich building contractor whose wealth had been largely created from government contracts for the vast programme of barrack building that was undertaken in the late eighteenth century. He was also responsible for the building of the Royal Military College, Sandhurst, and the Duke of York's Asylum in Chelsea. An associate of the distinguished architect Henry Holland, Copland had undertaken the

Gunnersbury Park at the time it was occupied by Alexander Copland.

conversion of the Albany Chambers in Piccadilly as well as the development of the Upper Cadogan Estate in Chelsea and the Tothill Estate in Westminster.

In 1801 Copland purchased land at Gunnersbury on which a recently demolished mansion had stood, which had been the home of Princess Amelia, a daughter of George II. Copland then built what is now the core of the Large Mansion, which was later extended when the Rothschild banking family took over the estate in the 1830s. At the time Adams lived in Ealing it would have been the largest landed property in the parish. Copland also had a town house in George Street, Westminster, and a further estate in Langham, Norfolk.

Although they met regularly, Adams did not record the details of any conversations with Copland. However, his description of a cricket match at Gunnersbury gives an indication of the latter's affluent lifestyle:

I could barely finish my letter to my mother and my journals before three o'clock when I walked to Mr Copland's at Gunnersbury. There was a cricket match of about twenty young men upon his grounds. They had begun at twelve o'clock. There was cold dinner served in a tent on the grounds between three and four, and after dinner the young men returned to their cricket. George and I were invited to the dinner at 3 and the ladies to a party after dinner at five. The morning had been unpromising, with some rain. But the afternoon was mild and dry. The ground under the tent was damp, and we had boards under our feet while seated at dinner. The greatest annoyance was a swarm of wasps, which were attracted by the good fare, and were buzzing round our ears, and ranging over the tables, during the whole dinner time. There were only men at the dinner. …

After sitting about an hour at table we returned to witness the match of the cricketers which continued until the dusk. The company then repaired to the portico, a detached building near the house where they have a billiard room – an elegant dessert was there set out, and the ladies, wives and daughters of

all those I have mentioned and some others joined the party. But neither Lady Carr, nor any of her family were there. I took a walk round the grounds. There are seventy-two acres enclosed within the garden walls. The walk round it is at least a mile and a half. The kitchen garden, fruit garden and hot house are upon a very extensive scale, and kept in the highest perfection. I was surprised at finding my walk brought me back again to the house. The company were just rising from the dessert; and we were entertained with fireworks, rockets, squibs, serpents and the like, over a piece of water in front of the portico. The grounds are laid out for a view from this portico in the most beautiful style of English ornamental gardening, with the distant prospect bounded by Richmond Hill and the adjacent country. … It was quite dark when the fireworks were over, and we repaired to the house where we found a new accession of company – among them were my wife and Ellen Nicholas. I played whist with Mrs Herriot and another lady and gentleman. The young people danced country dances until midnight.
(21 September 1816)

Major and Mrs Alexander Morrison

Mr Copland's near neighbour, Major Alexander Morrison, was a retired East India Army officer. Morrison was a long-time resident of the parish and occupied Gunnersbury House from 1805 to 1828. Major and Mrs Morrison were regular attendees at the various local dinner parties that the Adams family attended:

Walked an hour before dinner and dined with Mrs Adams at Major Morrison's at Gunnersbury. Dr Nicholas, his son Frank and two eldest daughters, Dr and Mrs Goodenough, Mr and Mrs Von Harten, Mr Copland, a Mr Ommany, with Major and Mrs Morrison, Miss Blair, and another young lady residing with them formed the company. … Major Morrison is a Scotchman, with the national attachments in all their force. There was music after dinner. The Miss Nicholas's played on the piano, and Mrs Morrison sung. The Major was enchanted with the Scotch songs. We came home about eleven. (12 October 1815)

Mr and Mrs Von Harten

The Nicholas, Copland and Morrison families met frequently with Adams and his family. During the early part of Adams's time in Ealing they were often joined by the Von Hartens. In fact, Mr Von Harten was one of the first people Adams met in Ealing:

But from breakfast time until past five o'clock, I was constantly engaged with company. Mr Hare and a Mr Von Harten, a German by birth, but a citizen of the United States, came and took passports. (1 August 1815)

Later, at Adams's first dinner at Dr Nicholas's home, he conversed more fully with Von Harten:

This gentleman asked me if I recollected having in the year 1809 met at sea, off the Orkney islands, a vessel called The Edward *of New York, … I had a distinct recollection of it. He said he was on board of that vessel. It is mentioned in my journal of 13th September 1809. He has since been to America, and is married to an American lady, a native of Fairfield in Connecticut. He has resided in this vicinity these two years.* (1 September 1815)

Two days later Adams writes:

Mr Von Harten paid me a visit. He lives at Drayton Green. He has a plantation and a partner in the Havanna. (3 September 1815)

In due course, Mrs Von Harten became a confidante of Louisa Adams:

Mrs Adams paid a visit to the Miss Nicholas's, and received visits from Major and Mrs Morrison and Miss Carnell and from Mrs Von Harten who was a daughter of Mr Burr of Fairfield in Connecticut. She made a runaway match from a boarding school at New York with an Englishman named Jenkins by whom she had her two daughters. After his death she married Mr Von Harten, by whom she has no children. But she wishes them to take his name, taking no satisfaction in the remembrance of her former husband. (3 December 1815)

We dined at Mr Von Harten's …The dinner was very agreeable, and would have been more so, but for a cold dining room. We sat late at table and had no music by the ladies after dinner. (21 December 1815)

By the spring of 1816 matters had taken a turn for the worse for the Von Hartens:

Mrs Von Harten is also very unwell with a liver complaint and strongly threatening symptoms of pulmonary consumption. She was much dejected and in an irritable state of mind. (17 March 1816)

I rode with Mrs Adams to the late residence of Mr Von Harten at Drayton Green. It was said there was to be a sale of his effects next week, but on enquiry at the house we found it was not so. Von Harten himself is in the King's Bench Prison, arrested for debt, and will go through a statute of bankruptcy. (30 May 1816)

Von Harten's business had evidently failed, leading to bankruptcy, and Mrs Von Harten now had to live in reduced circumstances:

Mrs Von Harten came from Clapham where she now has lodgings, and passed the day with Mrs Adams and dined with us. She is in great distress and appears to be almost in the last stage of a consumption. Her husband has been upwards of two months in the King's Bench Prison, and is going through a commission of bankruptcy. She expected he would be released this day. Their house at Drayton Green has been seized and sold. She was obliged to go at first into lodgings in the city, but found her illness so much increased there that she was again compelled to remove into the country and took apartments at Clapham. She told Mrs Adams this day the whole history of her life, which has been very unhappy by the misconduct of her former husband. It is now embittered by Von Harten's misfortunes and she is so much reduced that a very short time will in every probability bring both her sorrows and her joys in this world to a close. She left immediately after dinner to return home. (13 June 1816)

This final brief entry in the diary is the last mention made of the Von Hartens:

Mrs Adams went to Clapham and paid a visit to Mrs Von Harten. Her husband is not yet released from prison. (30 June 1816)

Beyond the Nicholas, Copland, Morrison and Von Harten families, Adams and his family had a range of local friends and acquaintances with whom they would occasionally dine. Some notable ones are detailed below.

Admiral Sir Benjamin Hallowell and Mrs Mary Elmsley

An Admiral Hallowell attended a dinner party at Little Boston and is mentioned as being at various local parties that Adams attended. Hallowell is described in the parish rate books as living in 'Ealing Town' (the old village around St Mary's Church). Benjamin Hallowell (1761–1834) had had a very distinguished naval career spanning the American Revolutionary War, the French Revolutionary War and the Napoleonic Wars. He was one of the select group of officers whom Nelson referred to as his 'band of brothers' at the battle of the Nile in 1798. After the battle, Hallowell gave Nelson a coffin made from the timbers of a destroyed French flagship. Nelson appreciated the joke and kept the coffin in his cabin – and was indeed buried in it after his death at the Battle of Trafalgar in 1805. Surprisingly, Adams does not mention in his diaries that Hallowell's mother, Mary (Boylston) Hallowell, was the daughter of Thomas Boylston and first cousin of Susanna Boylston, the mother of John Adams and grandmother of John Quincy Adams.

Living with Hallowell was his widowed sister Mrs Mary Elmsley whom Adams had known many years previously:

Sir Benjamin
Hallowell,
1833.
(John Hayter)

After church we paid visits to the Miss Nicholas's and to Mrs Elmsley … Mrs Elmsley is a sister of Sir Benjamin Hallowell and Mr Boylston. I had not seen her since the year 1796 before she was married. Her husband was Chief Justice of Upper Canada, but she has been these ten years a widow. (25 February 1816)

Mary Elmsley had returned to England with her family after the early death of her husband John Elmsley in 1805. John Elmsley had served successively as Chief Justice of Upper and Lower Canada from 1796 until his death. Because of this past association, Adams was evidently close to Mary Elmsley and the families were regular visitors to each other's homes.

The Roberts family

The Roberts were a long-standing Ealing family who lived at a house called Village Park on what was then known as Gunnersbury Lane and is now Popes Lane. Their extensive estates covered both sides of the lane and the footpath leading across their lands to St Mary's Church is still known today as Roberts Alley. Adams met the Roberts occasionally, but it was not necessarily an enjoyable or informative experience. Adams reports one occasion with pithy insight:

Took a short hour's walk to Brentford with George, and dined with Major and Mrs Morrison at Gunnersbury. … the company were a Mr and Mrs Roberts and a Mr and Mrs Welch, none of whom I had ever before seen, Mrs Von Harten, with Miss Carnell, Mr King, and the two young Clifton's. Miss Blair and Miss Ramsay are of Major Morrison's family. The dinner party was not very entertaining, for Mr and Mrs Roberts were two thirds of the time raving against Bonaparte and the French, and the remaining third, Mr Welch was almost equally violent against the Property Tax. There was of course nothing like rational conversation. Mrs Roberts, an elderly woman, was almost in convulsions of rage because they had not put Bonaparte to death, and her husband was in high admiration with the Pope, because he now suffers nobody to speak French to him. I asked him if it was the same Pope, who had crowned Bonaparte Emperor of France. He said yes – but that had been explained to him so that he could not blame the Pope for it. (12 March 1816)

Adams was obliged to socialise with Mr Roberts again after the cricket match at Gunnersbury:

Mr Roberts the Exchequer Clerk annoyed me a little by his impertinence. He is said to be a very good sort of man, but a ridiculous character who in his capacity of exchequer clerk fancies himself the very mainspring of this Government and Nation. He goes by the nickname of Pom among his acquaintances here for his dogmatism and self-importance. (21 September 1816)

Village Park in Popes Lane, 1903, the home of the Roberts family (H. A. Ball)

Dr William Goodenough

Another occasional attendee at dinner parties and a near neighbour of the Roberts family was Dr William Goodenough who ran a school at Popes Cross, which was adjacent to the crossroads between today's South Ealing Road and Popes Lane. Goodenough was headmaster between 1798 and 1818, having succeeded his uncle the Reverend Samuel Goodenough who had become Bishop of Carlisle. Goodenough House, as the school was sometimes known, was another of the boys' academies for which Ealing was well known. Distinguished former pupils included Viscount Sidmouth, the prime minister, and Thomas Bruce, the Earl Elgin of 'Elgin Marbles' repute. Most notorious was a former headmaster, the Reverend William Dodd, who forged a signatory note of a wealthy pupil and suffered the distinction of being the last person to be hanged in Britain for the crime of forgery.

Goodenough House School, 1848.

The Wright family

Curiously, within the small hamlet of Little Ealing there was another American-born resident. On one occasion when the Adams sons had their schoolmates over to Little Boston after school, Adams writes:

The boys had leave to stay till ten o'clock, but it was past eleven before the party broke up, and we sent them all back to school together, except Wright, whose uncle, Sir James Wright, lives in our neighbourhood, and sent for him soon after ten. Sir James is the son of the last Royal Governor of Georgia, and was born in America. (9 December 1815)

Sir James Wright Bt had inherited the title from his father, also known as Sir James Wright. Adams does not record speaking to Sir James Wright junior. This may have been because Wright was ill – he died in September 1816 at the age of 70. Wright and his wife had lived in a house, thought to have been The Hollies, adjacent to the Ealing Park estate, near the junction of the present Little Ealing Lane and Windmill Road, since 1799. They had taken over the property from his late uncle Jermyn Wright. The schoolboy Wright, also named James, succeeded to the title upon the death of his uncle Sir James Wright junior.

Windmill Lane, 1903, with the Hollies in the background, home of Sir James Wright.

Chapter 6

Ealing life

Adams and his family settled in well among Ealing society. Apart from exchanging visits with their many friends and acquaintances, they also made the most of diversions offered at the New Inn in the village, by local fairs, and events such as the cricket match described in Chapter 5.

Entertainments at the New Inn

A few months after his arrival Adams was invited to join a 'gentlemen only' dining club at 'Mr Laws' Tavern' or the New Inn, which still functions as a public house in St Mary's Road opposite the church but was rebuilt in 1897:

I shortened my walk, the roads being very bad, and after returning home went out again, just before six to the dinner. It was at the Inn kept by a Mr Laws, and seems particularly patronised by Dr Nicholas. There were six persons present, the Doctor, Mr Von Harten, Major Morrison, Mr Copland, a Mr Gifford, whom I had never seen before, and myself. Mr Gray was engaged in London so that he was unable to attend. There were some other gentlemen of the neighbourhood who had been expected, but had not been persuaded to come. There was some old grudge between them and Mr Laws, which Dr Nicholas is endeavouring to smooth down with some prospect of success. The dinner had been ordered for eight at seven shillings a head, and the wine to be paid apart. We had a very good dinner and fair wines, particularly the port. We parted between ten and eleven o'clock and the bill amounted to 17/6 a head. We agreed to meet and

The modern-day New Inn, which was rebuilt in 1897. The tall building on the left is the old Assembly Rooms.

dine at the same house again on Friday, the 13th of January, and ordered a dinner again for eight. Dr Nicholas is going in the meantime to Wales to visit his father, 86 years of age and now very ill, but he expects to return before that day. The party was social and agreeable, and I can join in conversation with these gentlemen on any topics other than politics, upon which when introduced I am of course silent. Mr Copland came from London to attend the dinner, and returned to town this night. (15 December 1815)

Adams became very comfortable in the company of the local gentry and actively enjoyed hearing the local gossip and learning of household customs:

A view of the rear of the New Inn and the adjacent Assembly Rooms in 1895. (Justus Hill)

Walk to Brentford and then to Laws's tavern to the club dinner. There were only Dr Nicholas, who got home this morning, Mr Gray and Mr Copland. Major Morrison, upon whom Mr Copland had called on his way from town to take him with him, had forgotten the club dinner of this day and had dined at home. Von Harten did not appear, nor any other of the gentlemen who had been expected. We made no agreement to meet again, but had a social and not unpleasant dinner – no politics. Dr Nicholas talked about his Welsh tour. He said nobody paid any rents in Wales at present. He had £300 due to himself for rent of an estate in Wales, of which he could not obtain a farthing. They spoke of Dr Bond rather slightingly, for scolding in the pulpit at his auditors for not having their servants to attend family prayers. I asked if family prayers were customary in this country. They said they were practised in the evening by four families out of five … and sometimes in the midst of a card party, they call in the servants, leave the table, hurry over the prayers, and sit down to cards again till 3 or 4 in the morning. We parted about ten o'clock. (13 January 1816)

Immediately adjacent to the New Inn were the Assembly Rooms, which Adams described as having just been built. These formed part of the New Inn, being linked by a corridor, and served as the meeting place and place of entertainment for the parish. This building still stands immediately south of the New Inn, the ground floor still being used as shops. Adams went there on several occasions with his family:

In the evening we all went to a lecture upon Galvanism, at Laws's tavern, by Ferguson Hardie, a Scotchman styling himself Lecturer to the Prince Regent. It was intermingled with recitations, declamations and imitations. … The lecture was entertaining and the experiments with the battery upon a frog, a rabbit and a sheep's head successful. He likewise made some chemical experiments, formed some soap bubbles, and exploded others. Turned green waters red and red waters green, mixed together many of the gases, composed a burning mountain, made spirits of hartshorn, and some other surprising things. It was over about ten o'clock. Dr Nicholas and Mr Carr [earlier referred to as Rev. Dr Carr] *were there with their families. Many of the Doctor's pupils and Mrs Riley's School of Girls filled Laws's new Assembly Room. We had called at the Doctor's for our sons John and Charles. As I sat next to the lecturer's table, he without knowing me, asked me to assist him in some of his experiments. Being afterwards told who I was, he apologised to me, for which there was no occasion, and gave me for my son George a small zinc pallet and a silver plate with a connecting hook to make the little experiment with the tongue. This entertainment absorbed the evening.* (29 October 1816)

In contrast, Adams found many of the functions he was expected to attend in London as the American minister tiresome:

Received this morning, under cover from J. A. Smith, cards from the Earl and Countess of Charleville and Miss Tisdale with a note of the Countess of Charleville at home … We have no acquaintance with these noble persons, and though obliged to them for their politeness, their cards and note were a melancholy signal to me of the recommencement of at homes and harassing winter parties. (1 November 1816)

However, within days, Adams has no hesitation in attending more local functions to celebrate the Duke of Kent's birthday:

I dined at the New Inn (Laws's) with a company of twenty-two gentlemen, chiefly of Ealing and Hanwell, on the occasion of the Duke of Kent's birthday. Mr Carr, Dr Bond, Dr Nicholas, Mr Millman, Sir George Campbell, brother of Lord Cawdor, an Admiral and Member of Parliament for Carmarthen, Sir William Beechey, the painter, Mr Clifton, Mr Fletcher, Mr Copland, Mr Westmacott, were of the company. After dinner we had the usual Toast of Loyalty, with the cheers, three times three, and a toast in compliment to me of the United States of America and perpetual harmony between them and Great Britain, for which I returned thanks. (2 November 1816)

Besides the usual local gentlemen there were two distinguished artists at this dinner. Sir William Beechey (1753–1839) was the portrait painter to Queen Charlotte and produced many portraits of the royal family as well as Lord Nelson and the actors John Kemble and Sarah Siddons. Richard (later Sir Richard) Westmacott (1775–1839) was a notable sculptor with a local connection in that he had attended Great Ealing School and had possibly been invited by Dr Nicholas. Among Westmacott's well-known works are the Wellington Monument at Hyde Park Corner and memorials to William Pitt, Charles Fox and Spencer Perceval. Westmacott also created the memorial to Ellen Nicholas in St Mary's, Perivale (see Chapter 5).

As part of the birthday celebrations a few days later there was a ball at the Assembly Rooms:

The two Miss Bollmann's came out from London, to attend the Ball at Ealing on the occasion of the Duke of Kent's Birthday. Mrs Adams had sent them an invitation. … At half past eight my wife, with Ellen Nicholas, and the two Miss Bollmann's, went to the Ball at the New Inn; Mr Smith, George and I followed them soon after. There were 162 persons present. The Ball was opened by General Wetherall and Mrs Adams. There were nothing danced but English country dances. There were two sets of dancers, each of twenty-one or twenty-two couples. The ballroom was new, and although so long since finished that there had been talk of having Balls in it at Easter time, the walls were damp. It was too small for the numbers of the company, and for ventilation had windows only at the two opposite ends. The company was collected from the families of the neighbourhood. Among them was Colonel Stapleton, whom I had met last November at Mr Copland's, and who went with Mr Bagot to America. He went to Charleston, South Carolina, from whence he has been about two months returned. The heat in the ballroom was oppressive until the windows at one end of the hall were opened from the top. But this produced a noxious draft of cold and excessively damp air, to which all the dancers were exposed. (4 November 1816)

The ball was linked to tragic consequences, which are covered more fully in Chapter 11.

Local fairs

For such a serious-minded man it seems a little strange that Adams should have visited the local fairs, which were known to be raucous and sometimes disorderly. However, he had a natural curiosity about English customs and being the father of young boys probably felt obliged to go.

Brentford Fair was a centuries-old traditional fair held in the market place

Brentford Market Square where the Brentford Fair was held.

in front of the present-day magistrates' court in Brentford High Street:

Walk with George before dinner to Brentford Fair. And after dinner again with Mrs Adams and George. We saw one of the shows, a double jointed ox, between two and three feet high, a sheep with five legs, an armadillo, a jackal and a baboon. We also stopped and saw several people looking through a magic lantern, the showman of which announced that it was a view of the burning of the city of Washington, by General Ross. He said there was not a house in that city but what was in flames. And his next show was the battle of Waterloo, where he said the British Army had lost thirteen thousand men killed and wounded. While we were listening to him in the crowd, I felt a hand making a plunge at my coat pocket, and was in time to prevent its getting in. This was another kind of British hostility from which it was expedient to remove, and we returned home. The fair is confined within the limits of the market square, and is frequented only by children and the rabble. It continues three days. (13 September 1815)

LRM

Brentford Fair, like many others, had a reputation for being rough and rowdy, with some rather brutal entertainments – the stocks, prize-fighting, cock-fighting and even bear-baiting – some of which may have disappeared by the time of Adams's visit. The nature of the fair drew complaints from many local residents, but it survived in some form until 1932.

A rather similar story surrounded Ealing Fair and Races, held annually for three days at the end of June, which Adams also visited:

I wrote however not more than half a dozen lines, being called away to attend the pony races at Ealing fair. The fair began this day and is to continue the two following. Mrs Adams and the children rode and I walked to the races, which were on Ealing Dean Common. I missed the first of the three heats by going first to Ealing Common by mistake. I saw the second and third heats, the last of which was tolerably well contested. (24 June 1816).

The pony races were held on Ealing Dean Common, a large area of rough ground

Poster for the races on Ealing Dean Common in 1818.

Ealing Races,

HELD ON

EALING DEAN,
On the 25th and 26th June, 1818.

Thursday, the First Day.

THE LADIES' CUP,
Value 50 Guineas,

To be run for, by Ponies, not exceeding 13 Hands high, the best of Heats, without Limitation of Weight.

A PRIZE FOR THE SECOND PONY,
Likewise on the same Day, to be run for

Another Silver Cup, No. 1,
Value 50 Guineas,

By Ponies not exceeding 13 Hands, 2 Inches high, the best of Heats, to carry 7 Stone, 7 lb. and 7 lb. allowed for every Inch under.

Friday, the Second Day.

THE WATERLOO CUP,
Value 50 Guineas,

To be run for, by Ponies not exceeding 13 Hands, 1 Inch high, the best of Heats ; 13 Hands, 1 Inch, to carry 7 Stone, and to be allowed 7 lb. for every Inch under.

☞ *The Winner of the Ladies' Cup to carry 7lb. extra.*

A PRIZE FOR THE SECOND PONY,
Likewise to be run for,

Another Silver Cup, No. 2,
Value 50 Pounds,

By Ponies not exceeding 14 Hands high, the best of Heats, without Limitation of Weight.

To start precisely at Twelve o'Clock on each Day. No Race on any Account after Four o'Clock.

The Ponies to be entered at the Red Lion Inn, Old Brentford, on Wednesday, June 17, from 10 o'Clock in the Forenoon until 8 in the Evening, when the Colours of the Riders must be named, and no Pony can possibly be entered after that Day.
N.B. The Prizes may be seen at the Red Lion, and will be delivered on the above Days.

☞ *No Suttling Booths allowed on the Common on any Pretence.*

Ealing Fair,

Commences *Thursday June 24, 1813.*

The following PRIZES will be Play'd for, on the GREEN:

FIRST DAY.

A WATCH, Value £2. to be Play'd for at Single-stick.
A SHIFT, to be Run for by Young Women.

SECOND DAY.

JUMPING in SACKS, for 10s. 6d.
GRINNING through a HORSE COLLAR,
For a large Leg of Mutton.

THIRD DAY.

Old Women Drinking Tea, for a Pound of Tea.
A PIG, to be Run for,
The first that catches the Pig and holds it to be entitled to the Prize.
A WATCH, Value £3. to be Play'd for at Single-stick.
A POUND of TOBACCO, to be Smoaked for.
To begin at FOUR o'Clock each Day.

Poster for Ealing Fair, 1813.

around the northern part of Northfield Lane (now Northfield Avenue). Pony and donkey racing were regularly held on this common, leading to the rather derogatory local nickname of 'Jackass Common'. Adams's error in going to Ealing Common was perhaps understandable in that there were several areas of common land in the neighbourhood, which also included Ealing Green, Haven Green and Drayton Green. The title to these commons was held by the Bishop of London as lord of the manor, and was transferred to the local authority in the later nineteenth century. Today, the old Ealing Dean Common comprises the small park called Dean Gardens, social housing to the west and allotments to the east.

The fair, held on Ealing Green, was quite a major event, attracting people from all over London. In 1822 William Cobbett, travelling in from the west, reported seeing *'in all the various modes of conveyance, the cockneys going to Ealing Fair'.* The Green then had a pond at each end and the space between them would have been crammed with numerous tents, stalls and gypsy caravans. Adams writes:

After a walk in the garden went with my wife and children again to see the shows at the fair upon Ealing Green. There are several of them but we went in only at Richardson's, where we saw a melodrama called the Turkish Heroine and a pantomime of Harlequin's rambles with sailor's song between the two. The whole spectacle lasted about an hour, and finished just at ten o'clock when we came home. The seats were at a shilling and at sixpence each. The stage was under a tent erected on the green and their house was quite full. They repeat the same performance three or four times each evening. (24 June 1816)

Among other entertainments at the fair were known to be the 'performing poodle', 'talking pig', '30 stone lady' and '40 stone man'. Somewhat remarkably Adams attended each day of the fair and races:

It was seven when I reached home to dinner and had not even time for a walk. The boys had been at the second day's races. After dinner we all went to the Fair. Saw a magic lantern exhibition at a penny a head, and Saunders's show of horsemanship, tumbling, tight and slack rope dancing, all in the lowest style. It was past midnight before we got home. (25 June 1816)

Evidently Adams was intent on taking every opportunity to attend the events:

Having no time before breakfast, the journal of yesterday engaged me so long that I could do nothing upon the arrears of the last month. It was the third and last day of the Ealing Fair. At 2 o'clock Mrs Adams and the three boys went to see the races. After four I walked out, the rain which had begun about noon, having held up about half an hour, but before I reached the race ground, it had begun again, and I was obliged to betake myself to the carriage … I was in time to see all the three races except the first, which had been lost by Dr Nicholas's son, Frank. There were three others but they were run with no great spirit. (26 June 1816)

Adams and the boys even visit after the fair and races had supposedly finished:

Before dinner I walked with George to Ealing and the Dean Common where we found that they were still running the scrub races. The booths at the fair were partly taken down, but part of them still remained for exhibition this evening. (27 June 1816).

The demise of Ealing Fair

In later years Ealing Fair changed with, as a contemporary writer recorded, '*the rough and ready taking possession*'. It became necessary to fence off Pitzhanger Manor to prevent damage and the local newspaper complained that the fair had become '*an occasion of vice and moral laxity*'. At the same time Ealing itself had changed, transforming into the epitome of Victorian middle-class respectability typified by its title 'Queen of the Suburbs'. It probably therefore came as no surprise when the Local Board petitioned the Home Secretary for the abolition of the fair. Despite a local protest at the Victoria Inn (still functioning today as The Grove) on the Green, there appeared to be no significant opposition to this petition and the last fair was held in 1879.

Ealing Fair in the 1870s shortly before its abolition.

The Adams family also ventured further afield for entertainment:

We all went to Covent Garden Theatre and saw the Midsummer Night's Dream with the pantomime of harlequin Fortunis. Shakespeare's play is decked out with a great extravagance of pageantry, according to fashion of the times, and is encumbered with a load of untuneable music. All which was necessary to carry it down; for there is no interest in the play itself – though it contains some of the finest flashes of the author's genius. It is reduced to three acts – much is left out and many insipid songs are added. The pantomime harlequinade is another of the remnants of bad taste, which both the great theatres of the capital must annually bring forth at Christmas time. (29 January 1816)

Chapter 7

Education and Great Ealing School

When Adams set up home with his family at Little Boston House in August 1815 one of his first acts was to seek out a suitable school for his two younger sons, John aged 12 and Charles aged 8. His eldest son George, aged 14, was to be educated at home by Adams to prepare him for entrance to Harvard.

On the first day in their new house, Adams writes:

I rode out with Mrs Adams to enquire for a school for our sons John and Charles. We went first to a place called Orger House at Acton, about two miles from our own residence, where we found an Academy kept by a Mr Mullens. We saw the house and enquired of the terms, but were not pleased with the result of our enquiries. We then went to the school kept by Dr Nicholas at Ealing, not more than a mile from our house, and which had been well spoken of to us by Mr Howlett. It is a large school of 250 boys, and we were so well satisfied upon enquiry and inspection of the school, the dining hall, and the bed chambers, that we engaged to send the two boys as soon as we can get them prepared.
(2 August 1815)

John and Charles started at the school on 7 August 1815, as Adams relates:

I took my sons John and Charles to Dr Nicholas's school at Ealing. The Doctor said that by the rules of the school they could not come home the first Sunday after their entrance; nor the second until after the morning service at church; and to return the same evening. Afterwards, once a month they might come home on Saturday afternoon to return Sunday evening, and occasionally they might come on Thursday afternoons, their half holidays, to return to school by eight in the evening. We could come and see them there every morning if we pleased. The Doctor mentioned the necessity of adhering to the general rules, as one exception would make another necessary, and it then became difficult to draw the line of distinction. In all which I acquiesced. I left the boys there, and then proceeded with George into town. (7 August 1815)

In the meantime, George's home-tutoring routine had already been established:

I roused George this morning at six, and we began upon the course of studies which he is to pursue under my own direction. He read three chapters in the French Bible, while I had the Latin Bible to follow him as he read, after which we changed books, and I read three chapters of the French while he held the Latin book to compare with it. I propose regularly to pursue the same course every morning. I began at the place where I was in the course of my own reading. At

Great Ealing School

Great Ealing School in 1809. (W.J. Franklin)

The school Adams had selected was Great Ealing School, a private boys' school thought to have been founded in 1698, which occupied the former rectory of St Mary's Church in St Mary's Road, where Ranelagh Road is today. It had an excellent reputation, especially in the classics, being regarded as comparable to Eton and Harrow, and would have suited the high standards Adams set for his boys. From the 1790s the school was led by three headmasters from the same family, with the Reverend Dr George Nicholas, the headmaster during Adams's time in Ealing, being succeeded in turn by his sons George Frederick and Francis.

Amongst its pupils who later became eminent were William Gilbert of Gilbert and Sullivan fame, John Henry Newman who later became a cardinal of the Roman Catholic Church, Thomas Huxley, the scientist, and Zachary Pearce, Bishop of Rochester (after whom Rochester House in Little Ealing Lane is named). In 1847 the school moved to the western side of St Mary's Road and was renamed The Owls. In 1874 it became a day school, and then in 1879 it became a school for Jewish boys. It subsequently began to decline and eventually closed in 1908 to be replaced by the residential streets of Cairn Avenue and Nicholas Gardens, the latter named of course after its long-serving family of headmasters.

the 44th chapter of Jeremiah. I gave him also Gibbon's journal of his reading to make translations of it into French. (5 August 1815)

I had begun to give him the exercise of translating from Latin into English. He translated the first section of Cicero's second Philippic. He has not been used to this exercise and performs it very indifferently. (22 August 1815)

At the end of August Adams writes:

George alternately translates one day from English into Latin and the next from Latin (Cicero's second Philippic) into English. I correct his exercises every morning after breakfast. He also studies Greek by himself and Italian with Pio. Barberi gives him three times a week lessons of writing and of fencing. (August 1815 summary)

Along with his studies, George's health was not neglected as he accompanied his father on lengthy daily walks whenever possible.

Dr Francis Nicholas outside St Mary's Church in 1846 in what is believed to be the oldest photograph of Ealing. He was then headmaster of Great Ealing School, having succeeded his brother and father. The building immediately to the left of the church is the school. The young Francis Nicholas, known as Frank, is regularly referred to in the diaries.

In what was to become a regular pattern of life at Little Boston, John and Charles were collected from school on Saturday 19 August at 2 pm, joining the rest of the family for dinner in the evening with numerous guests; these gatherings often included some of their schoolmates. On Sunday the family attended St Mary's Church where a pew was reserved for the use of the house (and another for the servants). Adams noted that 'Dr Nicholas with *his school constituted a considerable part of the auditory'* (6 August 1815). John and Charles were returned to school on Sunday evening after dinner.

The Adams family became very friendly with Dr Nicholas, a widower, and his family of five daughters and four sons. However, the Adams children still had to follow the school rules:

Dr Nicholas told us that it was against his rules that the boys should come home every Saturday to stay over Sunday – because there was a Sunday morning school for the Catechism and the Bible. They might come home alternately every other Saturday, and the alternate weeks might either on the Thursday or the Saturday come home to dine, and return at eight in the evening. (27 August 1815)

In the following October George decided that he wished to join his brothers at Dr Nicholas's school as a day pupil:

George has been desirous of going to the school to follow the studies during the day, and to come home to sleep at night. After breakfast this morning I took Charles to school, and George went with us. Dr Nicholas said he had a few scholars on that footing, who lodged at home. One of them was Wright, the nephew of Sir James Wright, who lives in our neighbourhood. Another had been Fletcher, the performer at the late Exhibition, who during the last year of his attendance of school had lodged at home. He made no difference for it in the terms of schooling, but such scholars boarded at his own table. George remained there, and from this day commences his attendance at the school. Mrs Adams took an hour's walk with me before dinner. John made an attempt to write a letter to his grandfather in Latin. Charles had written one to him in French yesterday. … George came home in the evening, much pleased with his school. (4 October 1815)

But George was not let off his home studies:

As the clock struck I left my bed. I was half an hour dressing, and at half past five I roused George. At six he began his French reading which takes from half to three quarters of an hour. He has a mile to walk to school, and must be there at seven o'clock. (10 October 1815)

George recites to me every evening fifty lines of Homer. (10 November 1815)

George's out-of-school studies included sharing his father's interest in astronomy:

Rose again and heard George read by candlelight. The morning was fine, and from the windows of my library we saw the moon, at the last day of her last quarter, and only 40 hours before the change – the new moon being at 11 o'clock tomorrow evening. We also saw Venus and Jupiter, both shining bright as morning stars, and nearly in conjunction – about ten minutes distant from each other. (29 November 1815)

Come December, the school start time was delayed, presumably because of the dark mornings:

I am engaged in hearing George read until full daylight and from that time until breakfast, assiduous at the journal. The morning school hour is already transferred from seven o'clock to half past seven and previous to the vacation will be protracted until eight. (5 December 1815)

The boys still had time for social life, often inviting schoolmates to their home to dine with the family:

I found George's company all assembled. His schoolmates Buttanshaw, Chambré, Hanney, Hamilton, Jackson, Patch, Sheaffe, Turner & Wright dined and spent the evening with us. The four Miss Nicholas's came to tea and we had music and singing by the two eldest, … Our sons John and Charles stay this night at home. (9 December 1815)

Another classmate of George's to visit the Adams family was Newman:

Mr. J. A. Smith came out from London and George's schoolmates John Newman, the Captain of the school, and Watson dined with us. (17 December 1815)

This was John Henry Newman (1801–1890) who would become one of the leading religious figures of the nineteenth century. It was in his last year at school that Newman took up a belief in evangelical Calvinism. However, his beliefs later changed and he became leader of the Oxford Movement, which believed in restoring to the Church of England many Catholic traditions. This led to his conversion to Catholicism and eventual elevation to Cardinal. In 2010 Pope Benedict XVI officially proclaimed Newman's beatification as a

John Henry Newman as a young man. (George Richmond)

step towards his canonisation as a saint. However, George's friendship with John Newman was relatively brief as Newman left at the end of the summer term:

Short walk to Brentford before dinner. John Newman, Thresher and Burningham, three of George's schoolmates, who are to leave the school at the end of term, dined with us. (9 June 1816)

School life was not all focused on dry academic studies:

I then went with Mrs Adams and Mr Smith to Dr Nicholas's School, to the fencing match. We were belated and found it half over. We found our sons, John and Charles, in the midst of an assault. Excepting our sons, Barberi has only four pupils at the school, Daniall, Patch, Sheaffe and Watson. They all displayed their improvements by fencing with Barberi and with each other. After it was over we went into the drawing room and heard Mr Gini and Miss Nicholas on the piano with singing. Gini is the music master of the young ladies – an Italian, and an excellent singer. ... At seven in the evening we went again to the school and heard a lecture upon astronomy, light and optics by a Mr Garrett. It was not very amusing and the Professor however skilled in the natural history was not very well-grounded in the language. His pronunciation was so bad that one could scarcely hear it and refrain from laughing. The boys specially showed some manifestations of being disorderly. It finished between nine and ten and we immediately came home. (11 December 1815)

...after dinner went to Dr Nicholas's School and heard the conclusion of Mr Garrett's lecture. Mrs Adams did not go. It was upon the structure of the eye, light, vision, catoptrics and dioptrics, finishing with a phantasmagoria. It was much more amusing than the lecture of last evening, and the boys were better pleased and not quite so disorderly. The Professor's language was as ludicrous as ever – 'Ladies and Gentlemen, vy is my coat black, and a sheet of paper vite? It all shows the visdom of our adorable creator.' His phantasmagoria was good, but not equal to that we saw last spring at Robertson's at Paris. He exhibited shades of the Emperor Alexander, the King of Prussia, King George the 3rd, Blücher and Nelson. The boys shouted and clapped their hands at the sight of all these figures. There was also a female figure, said to have been the late Princess Amelia. At this, and some other female shades, the boys clapped and smacked their lips, which Dr Nicholas disapproved, and said to me smiling 'Hear now those rascals!' The lecture finished again between nine and ten, and I walked home with George. (12 December 1815)

The end of term was marked by classical readings by the pupils and Adams noted that the boys *'acquitted themselves creditably'.*

Studies did not stop for the boys during the Christmas holiday, although George missed many of his lessons during the holiday because of ill health:

There was a fall of snow this morning which covered the ground, but it disappeared again before night. Mr Huxley, one of the masters at Ealing School, came and agreed to give lessons of writing and arithmetic to our sons during the vacation. I had at first thought of engaging him for three hours every week day, and keeping a school room for the boys to give them employment. But as he asked half a guinea a day for this, and teaches only writing and ciphering, I engaged him for one hour at a time, four days in the week – to begin next Saturday – at five shillings a lesson. (19 December 1815)

Mr Huxley was George Huxley who was to become the father of Thomas Huxley, the scientist and leading proponent of the evolutionary theories of Darwin. Thomas Huxley himself attended the school but his schooling was short lived because of his father's financial and health problems.

School started again for the boys in early February:

This day Mr Huxley gave his concluding lessons of writing and arithmetic to my three sons and I settled with him. It was also the day for them to return to school, but as the exercises do not begin until next Monday we have indulged them in remaining at home until Sunday evening. I walked with George round through Gunnersbury, Acton and Ealing; as we were coming back we met two stages full of boys returning to the school. (1 February 1816)

The normal term-time routine resumed though George continued to suffer from frequent sickness, which interrupted his early-morning studies and often kept him away from school.

The Easter holiday of one week was utilised in improving the boys' public-speaking skills:

The young Thomas Huxley.

Heard the boys speak their pieces which they are to deliver at the approaching exercises at the school. (11 April 1816)

Heard the boys speak again – Charles whom I took great pains to teach in Russia and who then really spoke uncommonly well has now run into several very bad habits, which if not corrected in time will totally disqualify him from all public speaking. (13 April 1816)

Astronomy was again a focus of interest:

In the evening, the weather being clear, I showed George the six signs or constellations of the zodiac, Taurus, Gemini, Cancer, Leo, Virgo and Libra, with several other constellations. We sat up to see Antares rise, at about eleven o'clock. The planet Jupiter is in Libra. We compared the visible stars with the charts of Bode's **Uranographia.** (26 April 1816)

At the end of April 1816 Adams laments that *'a great and unwelcome change is taking place in the course of my occupations'*. His many late nights due to social and cultural engagements, as well as work pressures, meant that he was rising

SCHOL. EALING.

ANDRIA TERENTII.

Junii 12°, 13°, 14°, 1816.

DRAMATIS PERSONÆ.

PROLOGUS.	..................................J. Newman.
	...............................F. Thresher.
Simo....	...............................F. Buttanshaw.
Sosia	...............................J. Newman.
Davis	...............................W. Sheaffe.
Pamphilus	...............................W. Daniell.
Charinus	...............................M. Thompson.
Byrrhia	...............................H. Burningham.
Chremes	...............................G. Adams.
Crito	...............................J. Watson.
Dromo	
Myris	...............................W. Chambre.
Lesbia	...............................J. Standen.

EPILOGUS... ......*Davus, Byrrhia.*

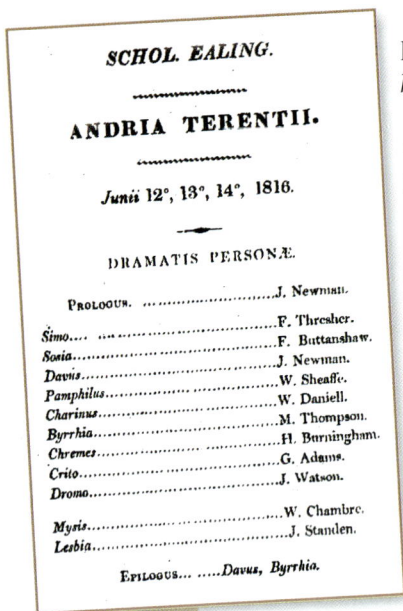

Programme for the school performance in which both George Adams and John Newman took part.

late or having to set off for London early so that he had *'ceased hearing George read in French altogether'.*

The end of the school year brings the school play in which George has a role and the family attended all three performances, as well as the boys' end-of-term 'declamations':

This was the first evening of the performance of Terence's Andria *at Dr Nicholas's school. We had intended to go only at the third and last night but while at dinner we concluded to go this evening. The performance began at eight and finished before eleven. George had the part of Crito. The whole performance did not quite equal my expectations.* (12 June 1816)

I was employed part of the day in hearing George recite his part in the play. We dined at five and in the evening I went again to see the performance. … The whole performance was much better than last evening. (13 June 1816)

At one o'clock went to Dr Nicholas's school to hear the Declamations of the boys. The Duke of Kent had promised to attend this day but sent an apology saying that the Duke of Orleans was to come and dine with him at four o'clock. The speeches were in Greek, Latin, French and English. Our sons George and Charles both spoke in French. … In the evening we attended the performance of the Andria, *the third and last time. It was much better than either of the former nights, and on the whole very well.* (14 June 1816)

At the end of June, Adams writes:

My three sons are now all at home and at vacation. They are to continue so through the whole of the ensuing month; but I can neither find nor make leisure to employ their time advantageously for themselves. (June 1816 summary)

However, during the holiday he clearly manages to make some time for furthering George's education:

George finished reading with me Terence's Phormio. (20 July 1816)

Fees for the boys' schooling appear to have been paid in arrears, and Adams is diligently prompt with his payment. In this extract he also records the likely forthcoming changes in his family's circumstances:

While taking my usual daily walk, I called at Dr Nicholas's, and settled with him the bill for the last half year's schooling of my three sons. He told me I had been the first last summer and was again the first now. It is one of the terms of admittance at his school that three months' notice shall be given before taking a scholar away, or ten guineas to be paid. I told the Doctor it was not improbable I might return to America in the spring, in which case I should take all my family with me. I wished him therefore to take it as notice now; that I should take my sons from school, if I should leave this country. He said that under my particular circumstances he should not take advantage of any shortness of notice, and he had seen in the newspapers that I was to be the Secretary of State under the next President. I told him that newspaper authority for anticipated appointments in America was not to

Education in England in 1815

In the early nineteenth century the few schools that existed were run by churches, private individuals or guilds and there was no great pressure for introducing a national system of education for all. The upper classes generally had no interest in advocating education for the working classes. In fact, there was a fear that education would take the people away from manual work and make them dissatisfied with their lot. Working-class families, for their part, were very reluctant to give up the earnings of their children at a time when child labour was common.

Education was almost exclusively under the control of the Church of England and the Church resisted early attempts by the state to provide secular education. A system of 'free grammar schools' existed which taught classical languages up to the age of 14. These schools were in theory open to all and offered free tuition to those who could not afford to pay fees. However, the vast majority of poor children did not attend these schools since their labour was so valuable to their families. There were also Sunday Schools, which were popular with the working classes as they did not prevent the children from working. By 1831, 1,250,000 children in Great Britain attended these each week, approximately one quarter of the population.

It was not until the Education Act of 1870, also known as the Forster Act, that compulsory education for all up to the age of 13 was introduced.

be relied upon, but various circumstances might bring me to the determination of going home the next year. (24 December 1816)

As the time for the family's return to America approached, George was allowed leave of absence from school:

General Boyd urged me to give my son George leave to go with him to Paris. His intention is to make only a short excursion, to visit Bruxelles as well as Paris, and to be back here in the course of three weeks. As George is very desirous of seeing France before he returns home, and this is a favourable opportunity to indulge him, I shall consent to his making this tour. (4 April 1817)

However, provision was made to ensure that John and Charles would not miss out on their studies when the family moved into temporary accommodation in London in preparation for their return to the US:

I told him [Dr Nicholas] I should leave our sons John and Charles with him until the time and manner of our departure shall be fixed. He renewed the assurance he had given me at Christmas time when I first gave him notice of our probable departure, that he should charge me for them only until the day when they should leave the school. (27 April 1817)

Dr Nicholas spoke highly of the achievements of John and Charles at his school:

The Dr spoke very favourably of John's proficiency, and said there was not a boy in the school who had made sounder and more rapid progress in his studies during the time he has been there than he had. Of Charles his report was also good, but being so much younger he is not yet so steady, nor is his mind yet susceptible of fixing itself so intently upon study. (27 April 1817)

Chapter 8

Church and religion

St Mary's Church, Ealing, c. 1770.

Religion played a very important role in Adams's life. He came from the New England puritan tradition but his views were not necessarily orthodox or narrow-minded. The choice of the Church of England for his place of worship may therefore seem somewhat curious. During their stay in Ealing the Adams family were regular attenders at St Mary's Church in the village. Later, when Adams was President, he would attend three services each Sunday, dividing his time between Unitarian, Presbyterian and Episcopal denominations. He seems to have been flexible about the form of religious worship and more concerned about understanding God's word and applying it to his daily life. Soon after their arrival in Ealing, Adams writes:

I hire the house in which we now reside, of a Miss Clitherow, sister to Col. James Clitherow, a Colonel in the militia. This morning, the Colonel sent us word that there was a pew at the church for the use of the house, and another for the servants if we should think proper to use these. We accordingly went to the church at Ealing. The church service was read by an old clergyman, Dr Carr, the father of Col. Carr, who married Mrs Perceval. The communion service and the sermon by a younger man. They were both very good readers. Dr Carr read a letter from the Bishop of London, founded on the recommendation from the Prince Regent to the Archbishop of Canterbury to raise a collection in all the Parishes of the Kingdom for the sufferers at the Battle of Waterloo. Dr Carr said that he should go round tomorrow to the dwelling houses of the Parishioners with the two Church Wardens, and he trusted they would contribute with their usual liberality. The sermon was from 1. Samuel 12.7. An exhortation to charity as cold as that virtue is proverbially said to be. The church was well filled, and Dr Nicholas with his school constituted a considerable part of the auditory. The beadle, who was clad in a showy scarlet gold laced livery, showed us to the pew, where we found two of Col. Clitherow's officers. There was however room enough left for us all. (6 August 1815)

Although Boston Manor House and the major part of the estate was situated in the parish of St Lawrence's in New Brentford, Little Boston itself was actually within the parish of Ealing, which was why the pew was made available to the Adams family at St Mary's. The vicar of St Mary's was the Reverend Dr Colston Carr who was then in his seventies and was to serve as vicar of St Mary's for 25 years up until his death in 1822. The younger man referred to was Mr Lewis, the curate. In his diary, Adams consistently recorded his views of the readings and sermons, making frequent acerbic comments about the ability of Church of England clergymen and the conduct of services. As an outsider coming from a more puritan religious tradition he often notes what he sees as failure to show a true Christian spirit, and the arrogance and self-importance of the clergy:

We all went to church and heard a Charity Sermon, preached by a Dr Crane before the Duke of Kent, for the benefit of the Charity School in the Parish of Ealing. … The Sermon was tolerably well written, and very indifferently read. Though a Charity Sermon it was not free from the tinge of an uncharitable spirit. For among the excellences of the Institution for which the preacher was begging he did not fail to enumerate its tendency to preserve the boys from the infection of methodism, or dissent from that most excellent and perfect church – the Church of England. There is something in the dress, in the gait, in the deportment, in the expression of countenance, and above all in the eye of these clergymen of the most excellent church, that imports arrogance, intolerance and all that is the reverse of Christian humility. (20 August 1815)

The Reverend Dr Colston Carr was a former headmaster and for a clergyman was relatively wealthy. He owned two other properties and had improved the vicarage to make it *'a respectable and commodious building'* according to a contemporary record. When Adams paid a visit to Carr he portrayed him as very much a traditionalist, particularly in his views of America:

I found him at home, and with a lady not in very early youth, his daughter. He is near four score years of age, and though in good health somewhat infirm … The old gentleman seemed sometimes a little embarrassed between the desire of observing civility to me, and the current in which his ideas have been running, perhaps all his life, but certainly more than forty years, in relation to America. He referred in the course of conversation to the American revolution and was about to call it the rebellion of the colonies, but softened his expressions with an evident effort, and called it the time when America was throwing off the yoke. His daughter, who had been at the fencing exhibition at the

The vicarage of St Mary's Church in 1876. It was demolished c. 1905.

St Mary's Church, Ealing

There has been a church on the site of St Mary's since at least medieval times. The old village of Ealing had grown up around the church and, being in the centre of the parish of Ealing, it was very much the focal point for life in the community. By the beginning of the eighteenth century the church had fallen into serious disrepair. In 1719 it was necessary to demolish the steeple and tower and by 1729 the church had completely collapsed. Rebuilding was a costly and protracted business and it was not until 1740 that the church was completed. It was this church, complete with a tower and cupola that Adams would have attended. By the 1820s the cupola had been removed and in the 1860s the building was radically redesigned by Samuel Teulon. Rebuilt in the Victorian neo-gothic style, it has a particularly striking if ponderous appearance, leading to Teulon being labelled *'a rogue goth'*. In more recent times Pevsner, the architectural historian, has described the church as being *'eccentrically elephantine'*.

St Mary's Church, c. 1910, after the radical redesign by Samuel Teulon.

school, complimented me upon the performance of my sons, particularly the two youngest. Mrs Carr, the Parson's wife, has been for some years nearly blind, and at the age of seventy seven was about a month since couched for cataracts, by the great oculist, Sir William Adams. (15 December 1815)

Adams assiduously recorded each visit to church and was particularly interested in anything unusual. Christmas was celebrated in a relatively low-key manner:

I went to Church with John, who was reluctant to go upon a week day, and pleaded that Christmas keeping was not a part of his religion. I wished him however to see the religious celebration of the day according to all the forms of the English Church, and in England. I had never seen it myself, though I had already passed two Christmas Days in the country, the first in 1783 and the second in 1795. The church was internally decorated with ever-greens, as are the Episcopalian churches in America. Mr Carr read the whole Christmas day's service, including the Creed of St Athanasius. The sermon was preached by Mr Lewis … It was one of the most indifferent sermons that I ever heard from this gentleman, who is here Mr Carr's assistant at £80 a year, but who is said to be going to India, upon a salary of £800. The church was about as well attended as it is usually on Sunday mornings, but nearly half its auditory consists of school-boys and girls, whose seats are now all deserted for the vacation, excepting about twenty of Dr Nicholas's pupils who remain all the holidays at his house. The communion, or as they call it the most comfortable sacrifice of the body and blood of Christ, was administered, but there were not more than ten persons who stayed to receive it. Mr Carr gave notice that tomorrow being the Festival of St Stephen, the next day that of St John, and Thursday that of the Holy Innocents, were to be kept as holidays and the Church Services would be performed. The clerk, Mr Atlee gave notice that this evening's service would begin at three o'clock, but I did not attend it. After church I walked round through Brentford, where the Christmas dainties were passing to and fro, about the streets, from the cook's, baker's and confectioner's shops. (25 December 1815)

These more secular features of Christmas in England were particularly noted by Adams:

This was the day of the Epiphany or Manifestation of Christ to the Gentiles, commonly called Twelfth day. Several of the shops in Brentford were illuminated, particularly the pastry cooks with a great display of their goods for sale. One of them had at the bottom of the shop a transparency with Britannia pointing to the inscription 'Glorious Regency'. About a dozen of the rabblement were collected together before the door and staring at it. (6 January 1816)

Besides the vicar and the curate, Adams recorded a number of other clergymen who administered services at St Mary's. One was the eldest son of Colston Carr, Dr Robert Carr, the vicar of Brighton whose close association with the Prince Regent led to his preferment as Bishop of Worcester. There were also various local teachers, Dr George Nicholas of Great Ealing School, Dr Charles Wallington who ran a school on Haven Green and Dr Bond who had a school in Hanwell. Another preacher from Great Ealing School was Dr Walter Mayers, whose evangelical outlook was to have a profound influence on the young John Newman.

Adams was generally dismissive of the abilities of all the preachers at St Mary's. His diary is littered with descriptions such as *'indifferent'*, *'below mediocrity'*, *'dull'*, *'inanimate'* and *'sluggish'*. However, Adams's particular derision was reserved for a Mr Milman who replaced Mr Lewis as curate at the beginning of 1816. At first Adams is prepared to accept that any shortcomings are the result of his youth:

The sermon was by a Mr Milman, a newcomer, a very young man, son of Sir Henry Milman and just entering upon his career. It was his very first performance. The sermon was very short. … With many marks of youth in the composition, there was good sense, reasoning, and eloquence, the promise of future merit. The delivery was bad both in pronunciation and in action, a canting utterance, a stiff and awkward continual shake of the head, and utter ignorance of the modulation of the voice. (14 January 1816)

However, as the weeks passed the diaries expressed a growing sense of displeasure as to not only Mr Milman's delivery but also his manner (Adams's spelling of Milman's name varies):

Mr Millman's discourses are not dull, for they are short and fanciful. He was more at his ease than last Sunday, which was his first performance. (21 January 1816)

Mr Millman's delivery and reading grows worse instead of improving by practice. (4 February 1816)

The sermon was preached by Mr Millman from Matthew XIX.17. The latter part of the verse … a discourse upon the necessity of good works, and the danger and absurdity of expecting eternal life, by means of faith, without them. Mr Millman's sermons have the advantage of being short. He seldom exceeds a quarter of an hour and he took no more this day to settle this mighty question. (7 July 1816)

Adams continued to record unusual events. At one service there was a marriage ceremony of a man who was apparently deaf, the circumstances of which were of interest to Adams:

Mr Milman also married a couple after the reading of the second lesson. The man was deaf and not prepared with his responses so that they had no small difficulty in getting through the ceremony. I thought it was the man's timidity. Dr Goodenough with whom I walked home thought it was obstinacy, which he said was not uncommon, when the marriage was compulsive, and made to save the Parish harmless, by the Parish Officers. Dr Goodenough spoke more favourably of Mr Milman's sermon than I thought it deserved. He passes here for a genius and has some pretensions to it. He has more imagination than judgement, and his learning is extremely superficial. (18 August 1816)

The implication from the remarks of Dr Goodenough was that this was an involuntary marriage because the bride was presumably pregnant. The groom evidently did not want to get married and pretended to be deaf. As the bride would have otherwise probably ended up in the workhouse it was in the interests of the parish that the pair were married. This interesting dialogue was however followed by the inevitable critique of Mr Milman. Towards the end of his stay in Ealing, Adams's dislike of Milman bordered on contempt:

The Sermon preached by Mr Milman from Thessalonians V.18 'In everything give thanks: for this is the will of God in Christ Jesus concerning you'. … All classes of his hearers were exhorted to give thanks: great and small, rich and poor, prosperous and afflicted, righteous and sinners. But the motives for their thanksgiving were not of the universal kind – but because they were not savages, because they were not heathens or Mahometans, because they were not Roman Catholics, of the Greek Church or Presbyterians – but because they belonged to the Church of England for religion, and because they were Britons for government. He did not ask them to give thanks because they dwelt in the Parish of Ealing, and enjoyed the blessing of hearing him preach, but that was the tenour of his argument. (17 November 1816)

The Very Reverend Henry Hart Milman as a young man.

Despite Adams's views, Henry Hart Milman went on to have a very distinguished later career as an ecclesiastical poet and historian. He became professor of poetry at Oxford, wrote histories of the Jews and of St Paul's Cathedral, and was a noted writer of hymns including the well-known 'Ride on, ride on in majesty'.

In October 1816 Adams recorded that his three sons were attending a Presbyterian chapel on Boston Terrace in Brentford. This chapel still stands and is now part of Brentford Free Church in what is today's Boston Manor Road. Brentford had a long tradition of non-conformity and the chapel can be traced back to 1683. The Georgian-built building that the Adams sons attended is now used as meeting rooms with a modern chapel next door to it.

The Adams sons began to attend the Brentford chapel regularly, while Adams and Louisa continued to attend the established church in Ealing. Adams passed no comments on his sons attending the chapel; presumably he was not only content that his sons were exercising independent choice in their form of worship, but that they were following the family's background of non-conformity. A few months later Adams himself attended the chapel:

The Brentford Presbyterian chapel, now used as meeting rooms for Brentford Free Church, c. 1910.

I attended with my three sons, at the dissenting Meeting House, on Boston Terrace. The services were performed there by a young man named Geary. The auditory did not exceed 70 persons including ourselves. The service was precisely in the same form as that of our congregational churches. A short introductory prayer. A chapter in the Bible read. A hymn sung. Long Prayer. Second hymn. Sermon. Third hymn and concluding prayer. The whole service took about an hour and a quarter. The sermon half an hour. … The sermon was written in a very good plain style, and the delivery was above mediocrity. This assembly is said to be so very small, because about half of the Society have left them and joined the Church at Ealing from unwillingness to share in their new Unitarian Principles. (26 January 1817)

However, Adams then reverted back to attending the established church in Ealing and once more was interested in a new experience:

I attended Church alone. The boys went to the Chapel. Mr Carr read prayers for the fifth Sunday in Lent, or Sunday before Easter. The Service was longer than usual, and was lengthened by the Churching of a woman, a ceremony seldom performed, for it is the first time I have witnessed it. (30 March 1817)

The ceremony that Adams witnessed was rather unusual in that it was a blessing given to a mother after recovery from childbirth. This ceremony includes thanksgiving for the woman's survival of childbirth and was performed even when the child was stillborn.

The apparent anomaly of Adams and his family attending a Church of England place of worship becomes more understandable from the diaries. Adams was an intellectually curious man and was interested in experiencing all the customs and traditions of English country life. The most obvious way to achieve this was by attendance at church, which also provided a means of becoming known and accepted in Ealing society.

Class and patronage in 1815

Adams came into a society where patronage rather than merit determined who got advancement in the army, the civil service and the church and it was mostly in the hands of the landed governing class. The standard of clergymen was consequently often low and Adams was routinely critical of the local clergy in his diary. Most of the population belonged to the established Church of England and it tolerated quite a wide variety of religious opinion. The upper classes undoubtedly saw the church as a bulwark against revolution. Protestant dissenters and Roman Catholics were tolerated but unable to hold public office.

Chapter 9

Social conditions

The stay of John Quincy Adams and his family in England coincided with a time of rapid social change. They were living on the edge of London, a huge city for its time of around a million people, and increasing in population as it drew in people from the surrounding countryside and also from further afield, including Ireland. The Battle of Waterloo in 1815 ended years of warfare in Europe and led to a post-war slump and an enormous public debt, widespread unemployment and hardship. Rural poverty and increased industrialisation were encouraging a drift to the towns and factories.

Adams was often shocked by the evidence of poverty in the country, as

Social change in 1815

Northern cities such as Manchester, the focus of the industrial revolution, were growing even more rapidly than London. The new canals had reduced substantially the cost of transporting heavy goods, and the increasing use of coal was linked to the output of iron, used in the manufacture of new machinery. The first steam-powered loom was set up in Manchester in 1806 and 12 years later there were 2000, making the cotton textile industry a large-scale mechanised process. By 1820 nearly half of Britain's exports were cotton goods, with America providing the raw cotton as well as being a major customer.

In 1815 one quarter of families still lived by working on the land and another quarter in crafts that served rural areas, but some people in traditional industries were being replaced by the new machines.

In lowland Britain the enclosure of land was completed by 1815. It greatly increased the production of food and also enhanced the position and power of the great landowners. But poorer small farmers, having lost their right to graze animals and gather fuel on common land, were often reduced to becoming day labourers. In some areas subsidies from the poor rate were necessary to keep families from starvation.

Conditions in the factories, which drew in many of the rural workers, were harsh. Children were widely employed, many of them pauper apprentices who were handed over to employers by the poor law authorities. It was not until 1819 that legislation fixed the hours a child over the age of 9 could work in the cotton industry at 12 hours a day.

Brentford 1848, one of the local areas where Adams remarked on scenes of poverty.

illustrated in many of his diary entries. One day's entry is taken up with incidents witnessed while he was taking his regular vigorous local walk:

I walked to Ealing and Acton, returning by the way of Gunnersbury. … as I passed by a small one storey house between Acton and Gunnersbury I saw two women, one of them with a child in her arms, standing before a window of the house and looking in. My attention was caught by hearing the woman with the child say 'Yes there is, as there is a God in Heaven! … There is a man there with a hat on'. She then shrieked, and the other woman screamed, and immediately two men and two women ran out from the yard of a house opposite.

The man in the house had perceived the woman as she first spoke, immediately jumped out of a back window and ran off towards Acton. There was no enclosure round the house, and only a gate opening from the road to it. The two men from the opposite house ran after him, but he had too much the start of them. A woman from a chamber window of the opposite house said she had seen the man go into the house – that he was a genteel fellow and wore a blue coat. The woman with the child it appeared lived in the house, which is scarcely bigger than a porter's lodge. She had gone out leaving no person in the house, and this man was a thief, who then at noonday went in to rob the house.

The woman was ready to faint and they took her into the opposite house. She said it was the second time this had happened. The man would have escaped, but just after he had got off, there came up a man in a light cart with a horse, who immediately turned round and raced back by the road to catch him at Acton. I then proceeded on my walk home and after passing Gunnersbury the man on the cart passed me, again, returning, and told me he had caught the thief, and that several things belonging to the house had been found upon him.

As I pursued my way home I met a boy of 13 or 14 standing beside a shabby little horse, who begged me to give him a lift to help him up. He had an old bag with some copper pence and half pence in it, instead of a saddle. These incidents lengthened the time of my walk. (16 March 1816)

Later Adams makes reference to more widespread social problems in the country:

After church we had a visit from Mr and Mrs Delafield who stopped on their return to London from an excursion of a fortnight into the country. Mr Delafield said they had heard great and bitter complaints of the distresses of the times, saw great numbers of poor people unemployed, sauntering about the streets and at alehouses, in idleness, and were told at one place that the wages of labourers were only one shilling and sixpence a week which the parish were obliged to make up eight shillings. (9 June 1816)

On the first day of July 1816, Adams gives an account of the illness and distress of someone outside his family and social circle – a stranger in fact. In doing so, he reveals something of the social and general health conditions of the time, as well as showing the charitable and caring side of his nature and that of his wife:

I was writing until past six o'clock, and then walked as far as Ealing Church. In the lane just behind General Dumouriez's house, I met a man with a very wretched and squalid appearance, with a girl of about twelve, equally miserable. He had an empty pint bottle in his hand, and accosting me, asked if I could give him a little elder wine.

He said he was a blacksmith by trade, and had been in comfortable circumstances and lived well. But he had been unlucky – had met with losses; times were hard down in Staffordshire where he had lived; and he had set out with his wife and two children, all that survived of eleven that he had had, to walk to London and see if he could get some work to do. He had come from Stone, 160 miles from home; and when he got as far as Brentford his boy, a fine boy about seven years old, was taken sick – he complained his feet were sore and that he could not go any further.

At first he thought he had overwalked the poor boy, for they had walked as much as twenty miles a day, but he had taken him in at Mr Baker's who kept a public house in Brentford, and there he broke out with the small-pox and was lying with it – very bad. The parish at Brentford had allowed him a doctor to attend the boy – but the doctor gave him very poor encouragement for the poor child. He the father had been round to every house in Brentford to see if he could get any work, but without success.

He was obliged to pay eight pence a night for the chamber where his boy lay, now entirely blind. He had sold most of his own clothes, and the gown off of the girl's back. The doctor had told him that elder wine would be good for the boy to keep his lips moist, and give him some sustenance, and he had now come out to see if he could beg any. I told him I had no elder wine, but gave him a shilling with which he could buy some, and passed on.

As I was returning from my walk, in the lane just before my house I overtook again the same man, with the girl. He thanked me very gratefully for what I had given him, told me his story over again, said he had not got any wine, … I told him that I understood wine was a very doubtful and dangerous medicine for the small-pox. But he said the Doctor had ordered it, and said any kind of wine would do, as it was only to keep his lips moist and to give him sustenance. I called the man into the yard, had his bottle filled with wine, and asked his name, which he told me was William Cook.

After dinner I walked with Mrs Adams and George to Brentford, and after being directed to three other houses of persons named Baker, we finally found that where this poor man and his family were. We left George below as he has only passed the process of vaccination. Mrs Adams and I went upstairs into the chamber where the boy lay, covered in a fearful manner with the small-pox. The chamber was not twelve feet square, with only one small window which was shut, and they had a fire at the foot of the boy's bed to make tea for him. Mrs Adams directed them to open the window, to have the fire put out, and to keep the child cool, without exposing him to take cold. And she told the man to call at our house again tomorrow. It was between nine and ten when we came home. (1 July 1816)

A few days later, there is more encouraging news on the Cooks:

W. Cook, the man whose boy has the small-pox at Brentford, came again with his girl, and told me the child was getting better every day. Lucy Hanel, the only person in our house who has not had the small-pox or the vaccine, was this day inoculated with the vaccine matter by Dr Cook's partner. (6 July 1816)

Adams records further episodes reflecting the wider social circumstances of the country at the time:

Five other men came from different parts of the country to enquire after work – ragged, penniless and almost famished. At the shop where we stopped in Brentford there was a woman who came from Basingstoke in the same condition. The distress of the country, about which so much has been saying these nine months, is just beginning to show here, in this shape. The colliers who were on their way to London, have been stopped by Magistrates sent out for that purpose, who purchased their coals, persuaded them to return home, and gave them money for their journey back. The effect of this example remains to be seen. The ministerial newspapers praise it as an act of great wisdom in the Home Department. (6 July 1816)

On the 9 July, there is mixed news on the Cook family:

The poor Staffordshire man, Cook, came yesterday and this day. I did not see him, but he says his boy is getting better every day. Unfortunately the girl has taken the small-pox and lies extremely ill with the fever. Dr Cook was here – Lucy Hanel's inoculation with the vaccine has succeeded. (9 July 1816)

The next day brings even worse news:

W. Cook came from Brentford again in great distress: his boy continues to be getting better, but his girl is much worse than ever the boy was, with a raging fever and at such extremity that he was obliged to go and fetch the Doctor to her this afternoon. The Doctor gave him very poor encouragement for her life and would not tell him whether it was the small-pox or not, for though she was taken sick on Sunday, there is yet no appearance of any eruptions. The Doctor had left some powders for her, but the old man said he was afraid the poor girl would not trouble anybody long. (10 July 1816)

On 11 July, Adams's forty-ninth birthday, he reflects briefly on wider matters, before recording further grim news on the Cook's daughter:

I enter this day upon my fiftieth year, and passed the day with the sentiments of gratitude for the past, of humble hope for the future, and of anxious concern for my children, to which it naturally gives rise. … As we were about sitting down to dinner W. Cook came in the utmost distress about his girl who he thinks will die. She is raving, and often convulsed, and there is a very slight appearance of any eruption. The poor man went to ask the Doctor who attended the boy, to see her this afternoon and he refused to go. Mrs Adams wrote a note to Dr Cook, requesting that he or his partner Mr Cooper would go and see the child. (11 July 1816)

Four days later, and it seems the immediate crisis for the Cook family has passed:

W. Cook came and brought with him his boy, who has recovered from the small-pox. The girl is yet very ill, but the pock have come out and are regularly filling. (15 July 1816)

On 24 July, there is further news of the Cook family. The medical position has improved, but it seems that the father is refused the opportunity of work partly because of fears that his son, who accompanies him, may be contagious:

Cook, the straggling man from Staffordshire was here. His daughter is recovering fast from the small-pox, but he cannot yet procure work and the people are yet much afraid of his taking his boy about with him. (24 July 1816)

Later in the year, we have further insights into the distress of some of the population, and Adams makes a telling observation on the wider social conditions in the country at that time:

LRM

The day was fine and I walked to Ealing, Acton, Gunnersbury and Brentford. In the lane from Gunnersbury down to the Brentford road, I saw a man decently dressed, lying stretched upon the ground by the side of the road, his face downward and apparently asleep or dead. There was in the adjoining field a man trimming the hedge of whom I enquired whether he knew anything of this person. He said he had found him lying there, had attempted to raise him up, but could not get him to speak. I asked him if the man was in liquor. He did not know. I requested him to come and repeat the attempt to raise him up. I then spoke to him and he answered. Said he was not in liquor but had a bad leg, had walked from near Windsor going to Lambeth to try and get into the Hospital, for which he had a certificate from a physician. He had found himself faint and laid down. Then I asked him if he was in want. He said he had eaten nothing for two days. By this time, two other persons had come up. I gave him a shilling and advised him to stop at the public house at Turnham Green and take some nourishment.

The number of these wretched objects that I meet in my daily walks is distressing. Many of them beg. They are often insolent and sometimes exhibit figures that seem prepared for anything. It is not a month since a man was found dead, lying in a field by the side of the road, between Dumouriez's house and Dr Goodenough's. Not a day passes but we have beggars come to the house, each with a different hideous tale of misery. The extremes of opulence and of want are more remarkable and more constantly obvious in this country than in any other that I ever saw. (8 November 1816)

Chapter 10

Walking the area

Adams seems to have been exceptionally dedicated to walking. It is clear from his diaries that he walks to an almost obsessive degree. Rarely a day goes by but that he records at least one walk of anything up to nine miles. He never makes explicit his purpose in such regular and lengthy walks. Certainly they would have given him valuable 'thinking time', but it seems likely that he would have also considered it a route to maintaining a healthy constitution.

Adams's walks enabled him to observe the everyday lives of those in his locality, including those laid low by illness and injury, and to muse on the

View of Robin's Farm from Popes Lane, 1895. This view would have scarcely changed from when Adams made his regular walks of the neighbour-hood.
(Justus Hill)

wider social conditions of which those misfortunes often formed a part. References in the diaries to walks also mention local landmarks that are familiar to Ealing residents to this day, and show his determination to continue with his walking regime despite injury:

I took a walk before dinner with George to Gunnersbury, and thence down to Kew Bridge returning through old and new Brentford. By treading on a stone, I sprained a sinew of my right ankle, which made it painful to walk, notwithstanding which I walked again after dinner with Mrs Adams. (21 August 1815)

From his note the following day it seems it might have been better if he had rested his injury rather than walking on it:

Found myself so lame this morning, by the sprain of my leg yesterday, that I could scarcely walk upon it. (22 August 1815)

But two days later he is off again and his walk leads to him making

Typical early-nineteenth-century 'short-stage' coach. (Marion Clark, after Thomas Moxon, *c.* 1838)

some interesting observations on the volume and nature of the passing traffic. He also comments on the consequences of unregulated competition between coach operators and the potentially serious impact that this competition could have on passengers:

I walked before dinner with George to Brentford and on the Richmond Road, as far as Sion House, the seat of the Duke of Northumberland. In a walk of about three quarters of an hour we met nineteen stage coaches, passing to and from London. Most of them loaded with passengers from twelve to twenty. The greatest number of the passengers is outside. They are generally handsome coaches, with the names of the places to and from which they go painted on the panels of the doors, and behind. They have four excellent horses, driven by one coachman, and fly like the wind. In many instances there are lines in opposition to each other, and races between the coaches of the two lines, which sometimes terminate fatally to the passengers. (24 August 1815)

Transport in London in 1815

The first surface transport in London for hire on demand – public transport – was the small horse-driven hackney carriage. The first documented hackney operated in London in 1621.

Larger carriages, or coaches, were being used for scheduled travel between cities by the second half of the seventeenth century, with coaching inns along the routes serving to accommodate passengers overnight and provide stabling and fodder for the horses, and maybe even a change of horses. Thus the journey was accomplished in stages, leading to the term 'stagecoach'.

Shortly before the arrival of John Quincy Adams in London, as the city had grown in geographical size and population in the late eighteenth century, larger coaches, similar to the long-distance stage coaches, had started to be used between the perimeter of central London and the outskirts.

These vehicles were called short-stage coaches, and could carry several people inside and others, paying less, outside. They could not operate in central London, because the hackney carriages had a monopoly on public hire in the metropolitan area, but they served the outer villages and towns such as Ealing and Greenwich. It is likely that it is these short-stage coaches to which Adams refers.

At the end of his first month in residence at Boston House, Adams summarises the pattern of walking which he has developed:

When I do not go to town I walk an hour and a half before dinner with George, and we dine at six. We take a second short walk of half an hour after dinner, sometimes on the neighbouring roads and sometimes in our own gardens. These walks however will cease with the summer. (August 1815 summary)

In December 1815, Adams is walking the full distance from his office in Central London to his home in Ealing, although his wife is unwell:

The weather being fine I ordered the carriage to come to the office at four o'clock. I left it myself at three with directions that the coachman should follow and overtake me on the Brentford Road. He did overtake me at the corner of the street from Brentford; but having walked thus far, I chose to complete the walk home, and came from the office to my house, nine miles and a few rods, in precisely two hours and a half. … Mrs Adams, who had been very unwell the whole day, found herself immediately after dinner so ill that she was obliged to quit the drawing room and retire to bed. (9 December 1815)

Adams starts May 1816 apparently still able – and determined – to find the time to walk the considerable distance from his home in Ealing to his office in central London, even though it would have saved him a great deal of time if he had taken a carriage:

Walked into London in two hours and 31 minutes. (1 May 1816)

After breakfasting with Mr Smith, George and I walked home. We were overtaken with a shower of rain as we came through St James's Park, and stood about twenty minutes under the shelter of the porter's lodge at Hyde Park Corner. This made us precisely three hours from the office in Craven Street to my own door. (11 May 1816)

Adams's entry for the next day seems to show a degree of satisfaction that he has improved his walking speed, despite hostile weather and at the cost of a minor injury:

At half past three o'clock, I left the office and walked home in two hours and twenty minutes, the shortest time I have ever taken for it and walking the whole way at the rate of four miles an hour. My usual rate of walking is 3½ miles an hour. I was twice overtaken with heavy showers of hail, sleet and snow – the first in Hyde Park, and the second at Turnham Green. The last soaked me through and through, so that on reaching home I was obliged to change my clothing. I had also blistered one of my feet. (12 May 1816)

Later in the month he decides, as he frequently does, not to walk the full distance from home to office, but rather have the carriage catch him up at some point and carry him the rest of the way. However, there is a flaw in his plan:

I left home at noon, leaving orders for the carriage to follow me in an hour, with the intention that it should overtake me at the entrance of Hyde Park from Kensington or in the Park. But it passed by me just before I came to Hyde Park Corner, and neither the coachman nor either of the footmen perceived me, although they passed me almost within call. I walked therefore the whole way to Craven Street. (23 May 1816)

Although Adams found the many formal events that he had to attend as American minister tiresome, there were occasions that he found interesting and enjoyable. One such was a river trip on the mayor's barge that he and Louisa were invited to join by the Lord Mayor of London, Sir Matthew Wood. This gave Adams an opportunity to view the environs of West London from a different perspective to that offered by his daily walks, and is one of the most memorable descriptions in the diaries:

At eleven o'clock this morning I was with my wife at Westminster Bridge where we embarked in the Lord Mayor's barge, but it was near twelve when he came himself with the Lady Mayoress and his family. There was a company of about one hundred persons … The barge was elegantly ornamented with streamers, and the Duke of Kent's Band of Music were on board. We started from Westminster Bridge just at noon, and were rowed down the Thames to Richmond, passing through the Vauxhall, Battersea, Putney, Kew and Richmond Bridges. The weather was fine, and the barge was surrounded all the way down by a number perhaps twenty boats filled with company, Ladies and Gentlemen, as witnesses of the scene. We passed by Chelsea Hospital, Craven House, which is the Margravine's villa, and some other country seats, as well as several villages on both sides of the river. But the prospects are not on the whole equal to my expectations. The country on both sides is very low and not remarkably picturesque. The Duke of Sussex and Lord Arthur Hill came on board at Kew Bridge. At Richmond we found the new, or Navigation Barge, called the Maria Wood, *in honour of the present Lady Mayoress. It is much larger than that in which we had come from Westminster Bridge, and the whole company passed from the one to the other. Just then the Duke of Cambridge was seen walking with Sir Carnaby and Lady Haggerston, and the Lord Mayor, accompanied by the Duke of Sussex, went on shore and invited them to come on board. They came accordingly, but could not stay to the dinner. The Navigation Barge was towed up the river to Twickenham as far as the Lord Mayor's villa, passing by Pope's House and Grotto which now belong to Lord Mendip, and several other country seats. We returned and anchored about five o'clock near Richmond Bridge, when the whole company sat down to an elegant cold dinner. The carriages were ordered to be at*

The Lord Mayor's city barge, the *Maria Wood*, built in 1816, pictured in 1863 near Richmond Hill.

Kew Bridge at eight o'clock, but it was nine before we left the table, and ten by the time we got back to Kew Bridge. The usual toasts were drank and the usual speeches made after dinner by the Lord Mayor, the Duke of Sussex, Lord Erskine, the Sheriffs, the Aldermen and Lord Arthur Hill and myself. …

There were some country dances before and after dinner, but the most delightful part of the entertainment was the songs and glees sung by the musical guests; which were without accompaniment of instruments, but in the very highest style of excellence. The Duke of Sussex sung a glee, Rosy Bacchus God of Wine, tolerably well. When his health was given the singing party gave the cheer of three times three hurra's in musical intonation, which was called for again and repeated. As the night came on the surrounding boats drew closer to the barge which was thus surrounded by genteel people looking in upon the company, and participating in the pleasures of the music. …

It was very dark when we landed, in a boat from the barge at Kew Bridge. We found our carriage there and were at home shortly after ten. (22 August 1816)

In December, perhaps spurred on by his river trip experience, Adams is showing greater enthusiasm than ever for his local walks, even to the detriment of his other responsibilities:

Having been shortened of exercise several days, I commenced my walk this day soon after two o'clock, went through the village of Isleworth, walked over Richmond Bridge, and returned along the banks of the Thames, till I came opposite to Kew Palace where I crossed the river in a ferry boat to Brentford. It must have been a walk of about eight miles, and absorbed so great a portion of the day that I had scarcely any left for writing. (9 December 1816)

Richmond Bridge in 1802. (Samuel Ireland)

Even on his final day in Ealing, Adams cannot resist the urge to walk part of the way to his new abode:

I dined alone and immediately after left the house, walked to Brentford where I was overtaken by the carriage. Mary Beach the house maid came with me. It was 9 in the evening when we arrived at the house in Craven Street. (28 April 1817)

Chapter 11

Sickness and health

A large part of the domestic content of Adams's diaries is taken up with health issues. Adams records everything from minor indispositions of family members, to major illnesses and excruciating injuries. He also shows his charitable side in helping those outside his family circle who have suffered health misfortunes and, in doing so, gives us a glimpse into the state of social welfare in the country at that time, which is described in Chapter 9.

It is perhaps unsurprising that such a lot of diary space is given to this topic. In a time before widespread medical relief and palliative care, when the use of effective drugs was rare, and when anaesthetic methods were unheard of (except for opiates), the threat of injury and disease to family life was an everyday concern.

Adams records a social event in Ealing which doubtless was supposed to provide light relief for the assembled company – a ball at the Assembly Rooms. However, Mrs Adams overexerts herself in the oppressively warm hall, and, when the windows are opened, the dancers are exposed to '*a noxious draft of cold and excessively damp air*'. Mrs Adams fell ill and tragedy struck another member of the party:

My wife danced almost the whole evening and before supper was announced appeared so much fatigued that I was alarmed lest she should be ill and gave her a caution. Supper was served in the rooms below, about one o'clock. It was just over, and a single toast, the Duke of Kent's health had been drunk, when my wife found herself so unwell that she was obliged to leave the table. Mr Copland led her into the adjoining card room, and we immediately returned home. Ellen Nicholas and the Miss Bollmann's went with us. We left Smith and George, who with the rest of the company returned to the ballroom and renewed the dancing till past four o'clock. It was after two when we got home. Mrs Adams was so unwell that she just escaped a fainting fit. But being put immediately to bed was immediately much relieved. (4 November 1816)

The following day he reports:

My wife had a very good night, and found herself quite well this morning. It was between four and five this morning when Smith and George returned from the Ball, and about noon when we breakfasted. … In the course of the day Caroline Nicholas had written to Mrs Adams that Sarah Carr, the Vicar of Ealing's daughter, had been seized with extreme illness after the Ball last night. She and her father, mother and sister were all there, and I had left them at the table when my wife was taken unwell and we came away. Mrs Adams sent to enquire how she was as soon as she received the note from Miss Nicholas. The answer was that she was as ill as she possibly could be, and was attended by Sir David Dundas and another physician. (5 November 1816)

Then on the next day they receive the news:

Dr Nicholas sent his compliments with the information that Miss Sarah Carr died at five o'clock last evening. We had invited Mr and Mrs Carr to dine with us this day, and their daughters to spend the evening. Mr Carr had promised to come to dinner, and Mrs Carr with her daughters in the evening. Dr Nicholas who was with the family all last evening and this morning again, sent us their excuses. Mrs Copland also wrote to my wife, requesting to be excused, having also taken a cold at the Ball. The rest of our company came. … After dinner my wife, Caroline, Ellen and Charlotte Nicholas, the two Miss Armstrongs and Gini entertained the company with music – performances on the piano and singing. It was one in the morning before they had all retired. The party was very agreeable. I had walked to Ealing and Brentford before dinner. (6 November 1816)

It is perhaps indicative of the relative fragility of life at that time, rather than any heartlessness on Adams's part, that Sarah's death is mentioned so casually and that the events of the rest of the day are then summarised without further reference to it.

In October 1815, Adams records an incident that was to have long-term consequences for his health:

I have purchased a pair of pistols for George and John to learn the practice of firing them, of their fencing master, Mr Barberi. As a trial of them was to be made, I chose rather to make it myself than that it should be made by either of them. Barberi had been running some balls for them. I asked him to load the pistols and said I would fire one of them myself. He mistook the quantity of the powder, and put in a full double charge. I fired the pistol at a tree in the garden, at twenty paces distant, but did not hit it. The pistol flew out of my hand and fell at least ten feet distant from me in a diagonal line to my left and backwards. It wounded my hand and fingers in four places. A lesson of caution for the children in the use of the pistols which I hope will not be lost.

Barberi afterwards fired the same pistol with half the same charge of powder, and it was still too much. The pistol did not fly from his hand, and the ball hit the tree, but just on one side and about ten feet high from the ground. Notwithstanding the wounds in my hands, I made a fair copy of my letter to the Spanish ambassador. (13 October 1815)

The letter to the Spanish ambassador was the last occasion on which Adams was able to write anything of substance for a month. The injury to his hand from the pistol incident seems to have been more serious than he first realised, and was particularly exacerbated by one of the wounds becoming infected. As he relates, Adams wrote

LRM

the diary entries for the month following this incident retrospectively, using brief notes written for him daily by his wife:

On the fourteenth of November after the interval of an entire month I am for the first time enabled to resume the pen. My whole course of life has been changed and I am yet uncertain how far I shall be able to return to my occupations. Mrs Adams has kept short minutes of the occurrences from day to day, from which I shall endeavour to preserve unbroken the chain of this journal.

This is the retrospective entry for 14 October:

One of the wounds in my hand festered in the night and was this morning quite sore. I wrote a few lines but the principal hurt is on the forefinger of the right hand, and I must consequently drop the pen for some time. (14 October 1815)

By a further cruel twist of fate, the injury to his hand means Adams spends more time reading than he would otherwise have done. This in turn leads to another ailment, which, if anything, is a greater indisposition and certainly appears to have been more painful. His desperation is made plain in this entry:

The incessant reading to which by losing the use of my right hand I have been reduced, has produced an inflammation in my left eye, which was noticed the day before yesterday by my wife, but to which I have myself paid no attention, until this evening on going to bed I observed that it was considerably bloodshot. My hand has been slowly healing and I expected to have been able to recommence tomorrow my ordinary course of occupations, and to have employed the usual portion of my time in writing. – Oh! blindness to the future! (23 October 1815)

The following day, it is clear that both writing and reading are no longer possible and his wife must now help out in both activities. Even his beloved regime of recreational walking now appears to be beyond him:

I rose this morning at the usual hour and heard George as usual read five chapters in the French Bible, comparing it as he read with the Latin Bible. … After he was gone to school I continued reading until breakfast time. But my eye was already much inflamed and very painful. From this time I was obliged to renounce both writing and reading. Dr Cook, a surgeon and apothecary of Brentford who attends the family, being here to visit Pio, whose hand is very bad, saw my eye, and advised me to diet and physic, to both of which I accordingly resorted. (24 October 1815)

Adams's affliction continues unabated the next day. The doctor attempts a diagnosis and proposes a radical course of action:

I had a night entirely sleepless; the inflammation and swelling of my eye continuing to increase, attended with severe and almost continual pain. This morning I could scarcely open the eye, and could not bear the light of day upon it. I was still in bed when Dr Cook called here, about ten in the morning. He expressed his opinion that it was the Egyptian Opthalmia, with a purulent discharge of acrimonious matter, and initiated the opinion that the vision itself was in imminent danger.

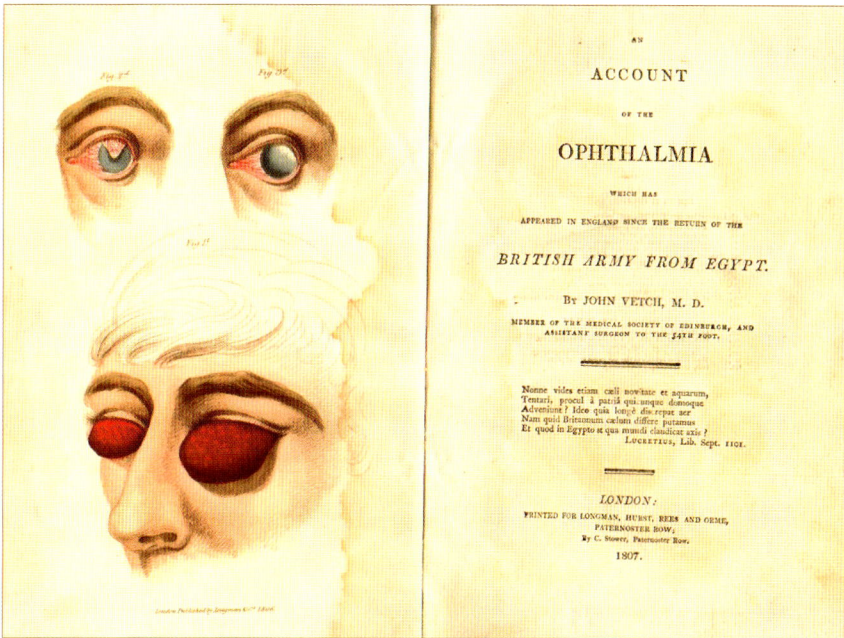

AN

ACCOUNT

OF THE

OPHTHALMIA

WHICH HAS

APPEARED IN ENGLAND SINCE THE RETURN OF THE

BRITISH ARMY FROM EGYPT.

By JOHN VETCH, M. D.

MEMBER OF THE MEDICAL SOCIETY OF EDINBURGH, AND
ASSISTANT SURGEON TO THE 34TH FOOT.

Nonne vides etiam cæli novitate et aquarum,
Tentari, procul à patriâ qui cunque domoque
Adveniunt? Idee quia longè dus repat aer
Nam quid Britonum cælum differt putamus
Et quod in Egypto et qua mundi claudicat axis?
LUCRETIUS, Lib. Sept. 1101.

LONDON:
PRINTED FOR LONGMAN, HURST, REES AND ORME,
PATERNOSTER ROW;
By C. Stower, Paternoster Row.

1807.

Egyptian opthalmia, thought to have been brought back from Egypt by returning troops, is described in this book by Dr John Vetch published in 1807.

I had better hopes, and told him that I had once before between five and six years since had a very similar attack, the course of which I described to him. He still adhered to his opinion, and advised an immediate application of leaches. He said however that he wished me not to be alarmed. I was however so averse to the use of leaches that he consented to wait a day or two longer to see if the inflammation would not subside without them. We tried the effect of physic, diet, or rather almost total abstinence, a hot foot-bath, and elderflower tea. I rose about noon, and returned to bed early in the evening. (25 October 1815)

After a brief respite, the affliction continues with renewed intensity, despite various attempted remedies:

I rose about ten, this morning, and the Doctor, who soon afterwards came, thought the inflammation of my eye had considerably subsided since yesterday and hoped it would pass off without making the application of the leaches or of a blister necessary. But the latter part of this day, the inflammation returned with double violence. The pain became intensely severe, and almost without interval. The physic, the foot-bath and the elderflower tea were repeated, and the abstinence continued apparently without effect. I suffered so much that I could not even listen to my wife's reading. (26 October 1815)

The pain and inflammation of my eye was so excessive that I had not a moment of sleep the whole night through, and it produced some feverish symptoms from which I had hitherto been exempt. My wife and her chambermaid Lucy Hanel were up with me the whole night. … When the Doctor came he reverted again to his idea of the Egyptian Opthalmia, and urged the application of leaches immediately as indispensable. I accordingly consented and about noon he brought and applied six of them to the swelling round the lower eyelid. Two of them would not effectually bite, but dropped off within five minutes. The other four bit keenly, and were nearly an hour upon my face. After they dropped off the wounds they had made were kept bleeding with continual fomentations of warm water between four and five hours.

My wife's kind attention was incessant but the fatigue, and anxiety and alarm, together with the hideous aspect of the operation of the leaches almost overpowered her strength. The bleeding by the leaches was so copious, that it very much reduced the inflammation, and gave me considerable momentary relief. … But … on returning to bed, the pain returned in all its sharpness. The swelling continued to increase, and the inflammation returned. I apprehended that the leaches had been of little service, and waited for the trial tomorrow of a blister. (27 October 1815)

I had a totally sleepless and extremely painful night. The inflammation and swelling round my eye continued to increase, and this day was so great that I could scarcely anticipate how it would end. … There is a discharge of a watery humour from the eye, the obstruction of which appears to be the cause of the inflammation. It becomes mucous, purulent and glutinous; and the swelling round the eye having almost entirely closed it, the discharge has been consequently still more obstructed. Yesterday the eye was often washed with warm milk and water, and a small syringe was used to wash the ball. This was found too powerful for the eye in its present state to bear. This day it has been frequently bathed with a small syringe, and the eye-lashes frequently anointed with lard, by a camel's hair brush passed over them. This enabled me to keep the eye open as much as the swelling would admit. Until this expedient was resorted to the eye was almost constantly closed by the glutinous humour which fastened down the upper eye-lashes upon the lower eye-lid.

About seven this morning I waked my wife, and requested her to send earlier for Dr Cook than the hour of his usual visit. I thought he would find it necessary to apply more leaches, and I was myself desirous of trying the effect of a blister. When he came he did not recommend any more leaches but agreed to send the blister. I rose about one o'clock afternoon, and it was then applied under my left ear. … The blister took but slight effect, and was almost imperceptible to me owing to the extremity of pain in the eye. … I went to bed about eight in the evening and the pain soon after became so violent that I was nearly delirious. It seemed to me as if four hooks were tearing that side of my face into four quarters. After being about an hour in that state, the pain abated considerably; the watery humour dropped freely and continually from the eye. The extreme swelling apparently subsided; and I could perceptibly open the eye wider than I had been able for two days. One abscess had found an opening at the corner of the eye-lid next the nose, and a thick purulent matter oozed out slowly from it. (28 October 1815)

By the next morning things are improving:

The idea that the crisis of the disease was past, and the relief from pain by the copious discharge from the eye, and gradual abatement of the inflammation and

Early nineteenth-century medicine

In the early nineteenth century, scientific medicine as we understand it was rudimentary. There was no understanding of bacteria as the cause of disease or infection and, generally, few effective remedies. In the absence of anaesthetics and infection control, surgery was a highly dangerous procedure. The eye infection that afflicted Adams was diagnosed as Egyptian opthalmia (also known as military opthalmia in the nineteenth century owing to its prevalence in armies). It is a contagious infection of the conjunctiva and cornea, producing pain, discharge and fear of light. If it becomes chronic it can lead to blindness.

The treatment Adams received included some of the standard approaches at the time. Blood-letting was an accepted treatment for all kinds of diseases and leeches were commonly applied to wounded sites in order to remove congested blood and promote healing. Regarded as something of a cure-all, leeches had been used in this way since Roman times, and in the early nineteenth century millions were bred for medical use. Adams was also subjected to 'blistering', whereby an irritant plaster is applied to the skin in the belief that diseases can be brought out from internal organs and dispersed.

A medicine chest dating from 1817.

Adams also mentions the application of 'physic'. This refers to a purging medicine or laxative.

By 1800, trained physicians were treating the better off and were available to the poor through charitable and voluntary organisations. But apothecaries and traditional barber surgeons were still providing services such as minor surgery, dentistry, dressing wounds and prescribing drugs. Apothecaries made up medicines and were also the main suppliers of leeches.

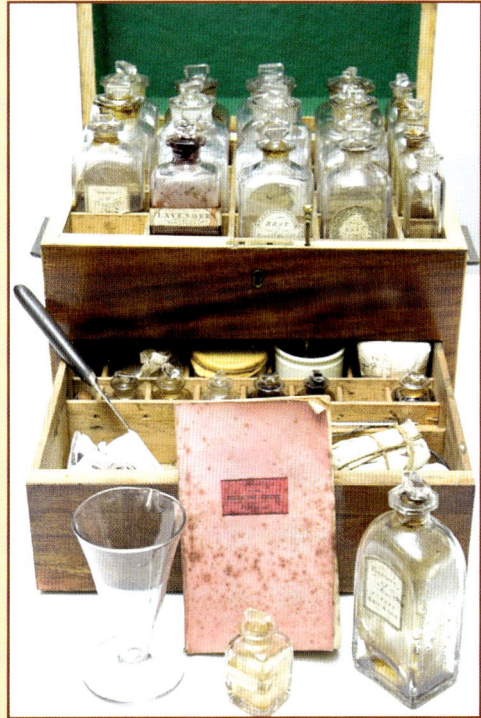

swelling, eased at once in a great degree my body and mind. The blister under my ear dropped off of itself, about five o'clock this morning. (29 October 1815)

Adams's recovery continues. But he vents his scepticism about the value of the previous medical interventions:

When Dr Cook came to visit me this morning, he found me so far convalescent that he said to me 'Well, Sir, we have saved your eye'. He attributes more to his own agency in this favourable turn of my disease than I think it deserves. That he mistook the nature of the complaint is certain; and I strongly believe that a more powerful application of physic at the first would have saved me from all its violence, and from the necessity of the leaches or of the blister. These did perhaps become necessary, and have been very useful; but it is not to the physician that I can give the glory of my recovery. (2 November 1815)

In his monthly summary for November 1815, Adams puts an optimistic slant on his recent travails and, surprisingly, considers that his general health has been good:

From the beginning of this month I have been gradually recovering from the severe illness with which I was afflicted at the close of the last, but the weakness of my eyes and the unsteadiness of my hand has hitherto made it impossible for me to write or read. I think that for the last thirty years, I never wrote or read so little in any one month as in this. As my general health has however been good I have been able partly to resume my occupations. My wife writes for me and reads to me. My rising hours have in general been three or four later than those of my healthy times, but the rest of the time is employed much as before my illness. I now rise occasionally at six o'clock, and I shall henceforth endeavour to retrieve the arrears of this journal. (November 1815 summary)

We have seen that Adams is specific and detailed about his own injuries and illnesses. He also refers throughout the diaries to the sickness of others, including members of his family, staff and acquaintances. However, in these instances he is notably briefer and usually unspecific about the nature of the illness, often simply saying they are 'unwell'.

For example, early in October 1815 we witness illness in the family, with all the children affected. Although the nature of the sickness is unspecified, it is deemed of sufficient seriousness to warrant the calling of a medical professional for the first time:

John was the whole day very unwell, and after church so ill that we sent for Dr Cook, the apothecary at Brentford. He came and prescribed medicines both for John and Charles. (1 October 1815)

Dr Cook visited the children again this morning: they are both better, but George was suddenly taken unwell at dinner and this evening was quite sick. He had taken a walk of five miles with me before dinner. (2 October 1815)

The children's recovery takes about a week. George appears to be particularly prone to illness:

George, in addition to his cough, is now afflicted with the rheumatism, and had this day considerable fever. (2 January 1816)

And the next day:

George's rheumatism increases in severity and this day he could scarcely use his hands. His cough however is less troublesome and his breast has been partially relieved. Dr Cook was sent for again and prescribed pill, powders and potion for him. (3 January 1816)

The following days see George's condition fluctuate, with new afflictions occurring as existing ones ameliorate. Adams notes that:

George whose rheumatism and cough are better has now a complaint in his legs which the Doctor thinks an erysipelas. He cannot yet leave his chamber. (8 January 1816)

And again:

I was at home at six; and found George suffering extreme pain with the toothache. Dr Cooke had been sent for, but declined drawing the tooth which he said was so much decayed that it could [be] safely drawn only by a professional dentist. (10 February 1816)

After several months when family sickness merited hardly a mention, in February 1817 Adams's wife is sick and confined to the house, if not bed, for virtually the entire month. Adams is initially unspecific about the nature of her complaint, although on the 7th he finally gives some details. The prescribed remedy is the familiar one of leeches:

My wife has been quite ill the whole day and this evening severely. She has long complained of a pain in the right side and it has become so sharp that this afternoon by the advice of Dr Cook she had seven leaches applied on the spot which drew much blood; at the stopping and turn of which she was in great pain and faint. She afterwards recovered, but remained very weak. I was up with her till near midnight. (7 February 1817)

Later in the month, Mrs Adams's condition worsens, and the usual grim treatments are applied:

My wife, who I hoped was almost recovered from her late illness, was again violently seized last night, and I found her this morning extremely ill with a high fever, and alarming inflammatory symptoms. Dr Cooper was here morning and evening and bled her in the morning. The abatement of the fever was but little in the course of the day. He left leeches at night to be applied in case of necessity in the night. I spent the day and evening almost entirely in her chamber. (21 February 1817)

Adams is more specific about a calamity that befell a servant of his neighbour:

Dr Cook came about eleven. He had been suddenly called to the coachman of our next-door neighbour Mrs Fisher, whose horses ran away with the carriage, and the coachman being thrown down in the attempt to stop them. The carriage wheels went over him, broke several of his bones, and left him nearly dead. (29 October 1815)

Adams does not make further reference to the fate of the coachman. (Mrs Fisher lived at Ealing Park, the largest house in Little Ealing with a substantial estate of 30 acres, which has subsequently been used as a school.)

In February 1816 Dr Nicholas is seriously ill and Adams makes a wry comment on the talisman which the school head had hoped would protect him from sickness:

Dr Nicholas is also extremely ill with the gout in his stomach, notwithstanding the magnet which he wears hung round his neck as an amulet against it. He has had great confidence in it until now. (10 February 1816)

Later in the year there is a further reference to a sudden, and potentially fatal, illness:

I went into London with my wife and George, who had been to Dr Nicholas's. The Doctor he said was very suddenly seized last evening, with the gout in his stomach, was very dangerously ill all night and not expected to live through the day. (28 December 1816)

On this occasion recovery is almost equally sudden. The following day:

After Church we had visits from Dr Nicholas and Alex Copeland. Dr Nicholas is almost recovered, and entirely free from pain. It was not an attack of the gout, but a sudden and very violent illness. They do not precisely know what. (29 December 1816)

Within a month, there is another reference to sudden illness – this time of a stranger – and an equally sudden recovery:

Walk to Hanwell and Ealing. Met a young woman who was falling into a convulsive fit. She was walking in company with three others, two of them young girls. I came up with them just in time to hold her up from falling to the ground. She was in a strong convulsion about ten minutes, when two gentlemen in a gig came up, stopped and offered their assistance. I asked them to let her be put into their carriage and taken home, to which they readily assented but she recovered so as to be able to stand and walk and her companions declined using the gig. She walked off with them. (31 January 1817)

Although average life expectancy was much shorter in Adams's time than our own, some individuals did of course live to old age. On 15 December 1815, Adams's diary entry refers to three people in their seventies and eighties. They include the nearly 80-year old Mr Carr, the vicar of the parish, and a local septuagenarian, the vicar's wife, whose eye problems must have evoked sympathy from Adams, given his recent experience in this area:

Mrs Carr, the parson's wife, has been for some years nearly blind, and at the age of seventy seven, was about a month since couched for cataracts, by the great oculist, Sir William Adams. The operation was at first said to have been perfectly successful but now Sir William says there is a film still to be removed from one of the eyes, and the old lady's nerves have been so shaken by the first operation that they have not yet ventured to tell her of the necessity of a second (15 December 1815)

And, most elderly of all:

Dr Nicholas is going in the meantime to Wales to visit his father, 86 years of age and now very ill. (15 December 1815)

Early in 1817, Adams makes reference to the unhealthy atmosphere in central London compared to areas further from the centre. This may well be one of the reasons Adams chose to settle in Ealing, rather than in the city:

Our company this day were all complaining that the fog had been this morning so thick in London that it had been scarcely possible at ten o'clock to see without a

candle. We had nothing of such darkness here. In general the wintery atmosphere of London is gloomy beyond that of any other place that I have ever inhabited, while within two or three miles of the city it is incomparably more cheerful.
(8 January 1817)

By March 1817, Adams has learnt that he is to be recalled to America, and has already transferred his family and many of his possessions to a house in Craven Street, central London, prior to his departure. The difficulties of living between two residences, and the forthcoming changes in his life, seem to weigh heavily on him. In his diaries he dwells frequently on physical ill-health. Now, his concerns are more psychological, although he finishes on an optimistic note:

Since our residence has been partly transferred to London there has been great entrenchment upon the regularity of my occupations. Late evenings and late mornings; frequent visitors received; many visits to be returned and continual interruptions of business; with a proportional waste of time. ... An unsettled state of mind with anxious anticipation of the future have marked a period of suspense, with alternatives all of which are cheerless, but accompanied with the hope and reliance which I never have had and have now no reason to distrust.
(March 1817 summary)

Chapter 12

Farewell

In the early part of 1817 Adams was waiting to be recalled to America. He began looking for a house in central London. Miss Clitherow had asked when they intended to leave. On 11 March Adams went into London with Louisa and took lodgings at 20 Craven Street, the same street where his office was located. Little Boston, however, was kept on with Miss Clitherow's agreement and there was a good deal of coming and going between the two.

The uncertainty about the future weighed on Adams's mind and he refers to being unable to work on several occasions. On 29 March he writes *'the double residence unsettles all my habits of occupation'*, and the following week:

I find myself not altogether well, and for some days past depressed more in spirits than in health. Every man knows the plague of his own heart – mine is the impossibility of remaining where I am and the treacherous prospect of the future – let me hope. (7 April 1817)

In mid April the uncertainty ends:

I received four letters. One from James Monroe, President of the United States, dated the sixth of March, last, informing me that he had with the sanction of the Senate committed to me the Department of State. He requests me in case of my acceptance of the office to return to the United States with the least possible delay to assume its duties. (16 April 1817)

Preparations for departure then began in earnest:

Yesterday a great part of our baggage, furniture and wines were removed from Ealing to the Consul's office at 1 Bishopsgate Church Yard and deposited there ready for embarking. (25 April 1817)

Adams refers to bidding farewell to many friends and frets about having to leave behind his substantial library of books:

The accumulation of books, pamphlets and papers in the course of eight years that I have been in Europe, becomes on occasion of such a removal, inconvenient and troublesome. Among the arts which are very useful to a person in a diplomatic career, is that of avoiding all superfluous encumbrance of baggage. I have had all my life a passion for collecting books, of which I now feel the vanity. I have not sufficiently considered that a great library requires a great house for keeping it, which it has always been probable and is now quite certain that I shall never possess. My library has scarcely ever been of much use to me, for I have no sooner made a valuable collection of books than I have been separated from them. It is probable that this will be my last removal from Europe; at least it is my wish to pass the remainder of my days in my own country, but I shall have at least one more great removal in prospect before the last. In the mean time I shall continue to be separated from almost all my books, and deprived of all time for seeking either instruction or entertainment from any books. (26 April 1817)

The Adams family library

In his will Adams requested that a stone fireproof library be built to store his and his family's books. In 1873 his son Charles built the medieval-style Stone Library next to the family home, the Old House in Quincy. It houses 14,000 volumes and other family papers.

On his final day in Ealing Adams writes:

We finally removed this day from Little Boston House, otherwise called Nightingale Hall, at Little Ealing, where we have resided since the first of August 1815. We finished packing up our baggage and furniture, and I had a considerable part of the day for writing. My wife went into London with Lucy this morning and sent the carriage back for me. I retrieved the three days arrears of this journal, and wrote a note to Miss Clitherow, enclosing bills for the rent to this day and requesting her to send a person to receive the house, and to examine with our housekeeper Mary Payne the furniture with the inventory which we received upon entering the house. I received from Miss Clitherow a very polite answer to which I replied by a second note. The waggon was loaded with our boxes and trunks, to be despatched early tomorrow morning for London. I took a turn round the garden, and bade farewell to the gardener Haig and his boy. Mary Payne the housekeeper and cook, and Caroline Hilliard the laundry maid, are left a couple of days to clean the house and are also to be then discharged. I dined alone and immediately after left the house, walked to Brentford where I was overtaken by the carriage. It was 9 in the evening when we arrived at the house in Craven Street. (28 April 1817)

Adams's final remark has a distinctly poignant tone:

I have seldom, perhaps never in the course of my life, resided more comfortably than at the house which we now quit and which I shall probably never see again. (28 April 1817)

LRM

Postscript

Life after Ealing

Adams was recalled to serve as Secretary of State to President Monroe, and the family returned to America in August 1817. A month after returning to the family home in Quincy, Massachusetts, Adams left for Washington. George started at Harvard and the two younger boys went to school in Boston. They were never to live again as such a close family group as they had done in Ealing.

Adams is credited with developing the Monroe doctrine which propounded support for the independence of American states while avoiding interference with existing European colonies or European wars.

In February 1825 Adams became President of the United States. He was described as upright and principled, respected rather than loved. Much of what he sought to achieve was thwarted by a hostile Congress. He used federal revenues to increase the navy, recognising its crucial importance to national defence. He was also responsible for building roads and canals, commissioning scientific expeditions and establishing institutions of learning. Some of his ideas were rejected by Congress, only to be adopted later: among them a national observatory and a naval academy. He oversaw the purchase of Florida from Spain. He served only one term as president, but in many ways was a man ahead of his time.

Adams served as member of the House of Representatives from 1831 to 1848, which was unusual for a former president. A fervent opponent of slavery, he was the attorney in the famous *Amistad* trial which tested its legality. The *Amistad* was a Spanish ship which, in 1839, was sailing from Cuba with a cargo of newly imported slaves. The slaves mutinied and forced the crew to sail north. It was intercepted off Long Island and the slaves placed in the local gaol pending a decision as to what to do with them. Spain demanded that they be given up and charged with piracy, but abolitionists sought to free them by legal process. A lower court decided the slaves should be given up, but there was an appeal to the Supreme Court, with Adams acting as the attorney for the slaves. He argued for the slaves' liberty on the grounds that the slave trade was illegal under Spanish law and 'natural right'. He won the argument, and the slaves were freed.

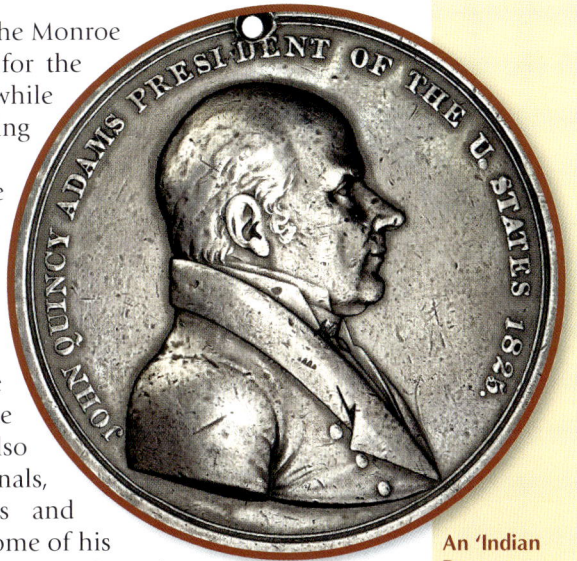

An 'Indian Peace Medal' showing Adams as President in 1825. These medals were awarded by US presidents to Native American tribal leaders as tokens of friendship.

It must have been a cause of great sorrow to Adams and Louisa that their two older sons died young. George died in a fall from a ship when aged 28. This may have been an accident, but it seems more likely it was suicide, as he had problems that would have weighed on his mind. He had run up debts and had a relationship with a servant girl who had become pregnant. Telling his parents about these problems may have been more than George could face. John also died prematurely, at the age of 30, probably as a result of alcoholism.

Charles, in contrast, entered the public service and, during the American Civil War, he followed in his father's footsteps by becoming Ambassador to Great Britain. While living in London he visited his childhood home at Little Boston and observed: *'I remember nothing since that came back quite so sunny to my heart'*.

John Quincy Adams died in 1848 after a long life at the centre of the historical events of his time.

The elderly John Quincy Adams, *c.* 1843. (Copy by Southworth and Hawes of daguerreotype by Philip Haas)

References and further reading

Baker, T. F. T. and Elrington, C. R. eds (1982) *The Victoria History of the County of Middlesex: Vol. VII: Acton, Chiswick, Ealing and Brentford, West Twyford, Willesden.* Oxford University Press. Available at: www.british-history.ac.uk/source.aspx?pubid=89

Brewer, J. N. (1816) *London and Middlesex: or, An historical, commercial, & descriptive survey of the Metropolis of Great-Britain: including sketches of its environs, and a topographical account of the most remarkable places in the above county.* Vol. IV. Available at: www.google.co.uk/books

Ferling, J. (1996) *John Adams, A Life.* New York: Owl Books.

Ford, W. C. ed. (1915) *Writings of John Quincy Adams.* Vol. V: 1814–1816. New York: Macmillan. Available at: www.archive.org/stream/writingsofjohnqu05adam#page/n7/mode/2up

John Quincy Adams, biographical notes. The Adams Foundation.

Morison, S. E., Commager, H. S. and Leuchtenburg, W. E. (7th edn, 1980) *The Growth of the American Republic.* Vol. 1. New York and Oxford: Oxford University Press.

Nagel, P. C. (1983) *Descent from Glory: Four Generations of the John Adams Family.* New York: Oxford University Press.

Nagel, P. C. (new edn, 2002) *John Quincy Adams: A Public Life, a Private Life.* Cambridge, Mass: Harvard University Press [Knopf].

The Diaries of John Quincy Adams: a digital collection. Massachusetts Historical Society. Available at: www.masshist.org/jqadiaries

Woodward, L. E. (2nd edn, 1962) *The Age of Reform 1815–1870.* The Oxford History of England. Vol. XIII. Oxford: Clarendon Press.

Illustrations

The authors and publisher are grateful to the organisations and individuals listed below for permission to use their illustrations. In particular, the authors are indebted to Lucas Reynes Matter, whose sketches have added a new dimension to the book. We have made every effort to identify and contact copyright holders, and apologise for any omissions.

Page 9: Photograph, LEHG.
Page 10 (upper): © 2014 Museum of Fine Arts, Boston.
Page 10 (lower): Photograph, Lucas Reynes Matter.
Page 14: © English Heritage.
Page 15 and cover: Photograph by Will Brown, courtesy of the Diplomatic Reception Rooms, US Department of State, Washington DC.
Page 16: Photograph, LEHG.
Pages 19, 20 and 21: Ealing Library Service.
Pages 22 and 23 (upper): Ealing Library Service.
Page 23 (lower): © National Portrait Gallery, London.
Page 24: © London Metropolitan Archives – City of London (http://collage.cityoflondon.gov.uk/collage).
Pages 26 (upper), 28 and 29: Ealing Library Service.
Page 30: Postcard, LEHG.
Page 31 (upper): © London Metropolitan Archives – City of London (http://collage.cityoflondon.gov.uk/collage).
Pages 31 (lower) and 32: Bellefeuille family.
Page 33: © Smithsonian American Art Museum, gift of Mary Louisa Adams Clement in memory of her mother.
Page 36: Photograph, LEHG.
Page 37: Reproduced with permission of M. Copland-Griffith.
Page 40: © National Portrait Gallery, London.
Pages 41 and 42: Ealing Library Service.
Page 43: Photograph, LEHG.
Page 44: Ealing Library Service.
Page 46: Local Studies Collection, Chiswick Library.
Pages 47 (lower), 48, 49, 51 and 52: Ealing Library Service.
Page 53: © National Portrait Gallery, London.
Page 56: Massachusetts Historical Society.
Pages 58 and 59: Ealing Library Service.
Page 60: Postcard, LEHG.
Page 63: Courtesy of Brentford Free Church.
Page 65: From Baines, E. (1835) *History of Cotton Manufacture in Great Britain* (Fisher, Fisher and Jackson).
Page 66: Local Studies Collection, Chiswick Library.
Page 71: Ealing Library Service.
Page 72: Courtesy of Marion Clark.
Page 74: Courtesy of Antiqua Print Gallery.
Page 81: Courtesy of Raymonds Press.
Page 87: Photographs, LEHG.
Page 89: Courtesy of Stacks Rare Coin Company.
Page 90: Image © the Metropolitan Museum of Art, gift of I. N Phelps Stokes, Edward S. Hawes, Alice Mary Hawes, and Marion Augusta Hawes, 1937 (37.14.34).

Index

Little Ealing History Group

In the year 2000, Ealing Fields Residents' Association, which covers the Little Ealing area of the London Borough of Ealing, decided to produce a local history book to mark the Millennium. A small writing group was set up and, in 2002, *Little Ealing: A Walk Through History* was published. Buoyant sales led to a reprint and the momentum to produce a second book. During the course of its researches, our group, now called Little Ealing History Group, discovered that future US president John Quincy Adams had lived in the locality in the early nineteenth century and kept a detailed diary of his life and impressions. This looked so intriguing that we decided to investigate further.

We started by obtaining a copy of Adams's copious diaries of his time in England, which were held as microfiche copies in the Bodleian Library in Oxford. Over the succeeding years, we transcribed entries that referred to our local area, or had wider historical interest, and arranged them by topic, adding our own commentary where appropriate. The result is this book. We hope you enjoy it.

Duncan Cameron, Andrew Dick, Paul Fitzmaurice, Helen Johnson, Rosmarie Matter, Joyce Mistry, Rita Smith, Mary Woods

www.littleealinghistory.org.uk